THE CASE

SBA FAILURE TO PROTECT 8(a) CONTRACTOR COMBATING FRAUD

Joseph N. Cooper

ISBN: 1470050595
ISBN-13: 9781470050597
Library of Congress Control Number: 2012902767
CreateSpace, North Charleston, SC

TABLE OF CONTENTS

Introduction   1

The CASE   3

The Argument As Presented To the U.S. Court of

Federal Claims   7

Statement of the Issues   8

Statement of the Case   9

      I. Nature of the Case   9

      II. Statement of the Facts   10

A. Background of J. Cooper & Associates   10

B. The Parties' Pre-Contract

Discussions and the Award

of the Letter Contract   10

C. The Execution and Terms of the

Letter Contract   12

D. SBA's Failure to Respond to

JCA's Multiple Pleas   13

for Assistance

E. The INS's Refusal to Pay Invoices   15

F. INS's Unreasonable Refusal to Issue   18

Task Orders to JCA

Summary of Argument   25

1. The INS Breached the Contract by Failing to Fulfill

Its Contractual Duties to JCA   27

A. The INS Breached the Contract by Ordering
Advertising Services Identified in the Requirement
from Contractors Other Than JCA   27

1. The Letter Contract Is a Requirements Contract   28

2. The INS Procured Advertising Services Identified
in the Requirement from Contractors Other Than JCA   30

B. The INS Breached the Contract by Failing
to Cooperate with JCA and by Acting in Violation of
Federal Procurement Law   30

1. The INS Failed to Cooperate with JCA   31

2. The INS Violated Federal Procurement Laws to
Evade Its Contract with JCA   33

a. The INS Violated the FAR by Using BPAs to
Order Services for the Requirement   34

b. The INS Violated the FAR by Its Failure to Notify the SBA
that the INS Had Ordered Services for the Requirement
from Non-8(a) Contractors   35

C. The INS Breached the Contract by Its
Prolonged Failure to Pay JCA   37

1. The Government Has Contractual Duty to Pay JCA   37

2. The Government Failed to Pay JCA   37

1. The Government Unilaterally Reduced
Agreed-upon Labor Rates   39

II.   The SBA Breached Its Contract with JCA by Failing
to Fulfill the SBA's Contractual Duties to JCA   39

A. The SBA Breached its Contractual Duties to JCA
by Failing to Fulfill Duties Expressly Imposed by its
Enabling Statute and Implementing Regulations   40
1. The SBA Breached the Contract by Failing to Aid and
Assist JCA and Failing to Protect JCA's Interests in Its
Dealing with the INS   40
2.   The SBA Failed to Ensure that the Task Orders Issued by
the INS under the Contract Were "Fair and Reasonable,"
and Represented a "Fair Market Price"   44
B. The SBA Breached Its Implied Contractual Duties to
JCA by the SBA's Unreasonable Failure to Cooperate with
JCA to Respond to JCA's Repeated Requests for Assistance   47

U.S. COURT OF FEDERAL CLAIMS FILED: JULY 12, 2002   49
    IDIQ CONTRACT   51
    DISSATISFIED WITH JCA PERFORMANCE   53
    JOSEPH GARFORTH DEPOSITION   54
    JCA's PRICING   56
    ONE LAST CHANCE   57
DCAA-JCA ACCOUNTING SYSTEM   58
INS WAS NOT OBLIGATED TO NOTIFY
JCA/INS WAS USING NON-8(a) FIRMS   61
U.S. DISTRICT COURT FOR THE DISTRICT OF COLUMBIA   66
    ORIGINAL SOURCE   68
    COURT STATEMENTS   69
FEDERAL ACQUISITION REGULATIONS (FAR)   71
BPA-INS VIOLATION: 72

BUSINESS OPPORTUNITY DEVELOPMENT REFORM
ACT OF 1988 (P.L. 100-656)   73
INS VIOLATED SET-ASIDE REQUIREMENT USE OF BPA   74
PAT COLLINS DEPOSITION   75
SBA FAILURE TO ENFORCE FAR REGULATIONS AND
SBA's POLICIES   78
CONCLUSION-FAR FACTS   81

IT's STILL GOING ON TODAY   81
LEGISLATIVE AND EXECUTIVE BRANCHES OF
GOVERNMENT FAIL TO ACT   83
CHANGE IS NECESSARY   85
COOPER's FINAL THOUGHTS   89

TABLE OF AUTHORITIES COURT CASES   91
AGENCY BOARD CASES   93
STATUTES, RULES AND REGULATIONS   93
MISCELLANEOUS   94
RESOURCE   95

SUPPORTING DOCUMENTATION   97

JOHN RUSSO'S LETTER MAY 16, 1996   98-99
BLANKET PURCHASING AGREEMENT – DATED 03/22/96 –
SIGNED BY LESA P. SCOTT   100
BLANKET PURCHASING AGREEMENT – DATED 11/13/95 –
SIGNED BY BETTY JOHNSON   101-102
MICHELLE WALL LETTER – DATED JULY 7, 1995,
TO SBA PATRICIA COLLINS   103-104

DEPARTMENT OF JUSTICE MEMORANDUM OF INVESTIGATION –
DATED JULY 15, 1997   105-106
NY TIMES ARTICLE – DATED 27TH, 2006   107-111
RICHARD POLLET, VICE PRESIDENT JWT LETTER –
DATED JAN 16, 2007   112-114

INTRODUCTION

The Small Business Administration's inspector general, Peggie E. Gustafson, while testifying in a congressional hearing last week, said that her agency often did not effectively oversee the contracting program and did not aggressively pursue companies that misrepresented themselves as small. The SBA, Ms. Gustafson said in her prepared statement, "needs to change its culture so that employees understand that their mission includes not only assisting small businesses but also ensuring accountability and integrity to prevent fraudulent and improper actions from depriving procurement opportunities for legitimate firms" [New York Times, November 1, 2011].

My case started and ended with the decision of Judge Marian Blank Horn, U.S. Court of Federal Claims. Her failure to examine the facts and evidence in my case was disgraceful and set the tone for how the government judged my case for assistance. In all the avenues that I sought help from—both government and non-government sources—I was rejected and told nothing could be done because of Judge Horn's decision.

We live in a civilized society. We give our courts a great deal of responsibility to be objective and fair when it comes to the law. When that does not happen, we experience destruction, and we question our courts and our system of government. There isn't any question—Judge Horn did not consider the Business Opportunity Development Reform Act of 1988 (P.L. 100-656); she did not consider the FAR Regulations, and she did not consider the SBA regulations and policies related to the SBA 8(a) programs. The INS and SBA lied to the courts about JCA, and the courts never questioned or requested backup documentation from the government that supported their position; Judge Horn accepted, whatever the government had to say.

THE CASE

The CASE is a story of how the Small Business Administration and Immigration Naturalization Service destroyed an SBA 8(a) contractor by allowing its contract to be taken away and given to big companies—J. Walter Thompson, Bernard Hodes Group, and CASS Communications—representing themselves as small, "disadvantaged" businesses, when, in fact, they were not. JCA was a victim of agency procurement officials who ignored clear violations of Federal procurement law to avoid working with JCA.

The strength of my case centers around the revelations that the INS program staff and Contracting Officials both knew or had reasoned to know that JCA's competitors had falsely certified themselves as small, disadvantaged businesses, but the officials repeatedly contracted with those competitors to JCA detriment.

My case had two major weaknesses. First, INS used an IDIQ contracting vehicle (Indefinite Delivery, Indefinite Quantity), which was structured in a manner that (1) imposed extraordinary risk upon a small contractor and (2) afforded the INS the legal right to abandon the contract with excessive ease.

Second, the law at that time had been long misapplied in a manner that permitted the government contracting officials to violate their duty to contract in good faith and to deal fairly with contractors.

The book discusses in great detail the specific laws and FAR regulations that the government and contractors violated to acquire contracts set aside for JCA under the SBA 8(a) program. It also discusses how the SBA did nothing to correct the problems JCA was experiencing with its INS contract.

The CASE discusses the decision of the two courts that ruled in this case. One of them clearly did not consider all the evidence submitted for review, and the other states, "The government's decision to award contracts to the defendants, despite its knowledge that the defendants were not small or disadvantaged businesses, negates any claim of fraud against the defendants." Finally, the one law that all lawful authorities involved in JCA's case (DOJ IG, SBA IG, U.S. Claims Court, and U.S. District Court) refuse to discuss or comment on is the Business Opportunity Development Reform Act of 1988 (P.L. 100-656). This piece of legislation addresses the heart of this issue, yet not one corporation has ever been prosecuted for misrepresenting themselves as a small, disadvantaged business. It would appear that the government doesn't have the will to take on big businesses in this area. The SBA has done nothing to address the problem to date. I have asked myself so many questions—none more important than "How long must JCA wait for justice?"

According to the American Small Business League and the U.S. Congress, small businesses across the nation are losing contracts that were legally set aside for legitimate small businesses, due to large corporations fraudulently misrepresenting themselves as small businesses. By failing to hold J. Walter Thompson, Bernard Hodes, and CASS Communications and SBA accountable, a message has been sent to the contracting community that there is no punishment for committing fraud. There is a need to put into place a mechanism to ensure that what happened to JCA will never again happen to another small business contractor.

For many years, I have wondered why SBA ignored the law and regulations involving JCA's INS contract. Was it due to incompetency, or was it calculated? I believe that the real problem with the SBA was that although it had the legal authority to compel the contracting agencies to fulfill their proper obligations to SBA contractors, it chose to be selective in whom it helped. Of course, I could be wrong, and they just chose not to help JCA for reasons I shall never know.

What I do know is that by any proper standard, the INS, a federal executive agency, engaged in patently unscrupulous conduct under its contract with JCA. The law at that time, however, provided JCA no remedy. In such instances, Congress has the power to provide "equitable" relief to contractors who have clearly been wronged but have no legal remedy. Congress, however, apparently decided not to exercise that power on behalf of JCA.

THE CASE

ARGUMENT

AS

PRESENTED TO THE

U.S. COURT OF FEDERAL CLAIMS

STATEMENT OF THE ISSUES

A.   Whether the letter contract was a requirements contract.

B.   Whether defendant Immigration and Naturalization Service ("INS") breached the letter contract by purchasing services from contractors other than JCA.

C.   Whether defendant INS breached the letter contract, both by failing to pay the amounts due to plaintiff under the letter contract for periods exceeding up to one year and by unilaterally reducing the agreed-upon labor rates.

D.   Whether defendant INS breached the letter contract by its failure to cooperate with plaintiff by ordering services from contractors other than plaintiff in violation of federal procurement laws and committing other violations of federal procurement laws to evade its contract with plaintiff.

E.   Whether defendant Small Business Administration ("SBA") breached the letter contract when it failed to fulfill its statutory and regulatory duties under the contract to aid and assist plaintiff and to ensure that plaintiff received fair and reasonable treatment from defendant INS.

F.   Whether defendant SBA breached the contract with plaintiff when it failed to cooperate with plaintiff in the performance of the contract.

STATEMENT OF THE CASE

I.   Nature of the Case

This case is borne of the tripartite contractual relationship among plaintiff, JCA, and defendants, the SBA and the INS. A three-party contractual relationship is mandated for all government contracts awarded through the SBA's Section 8(a) Program for small and disadvantaged businesses ("SDB") such as JCA. JCA brings this action because, in the current case, the tripartite relationship went awry.

JCA will show that (1) the letter contract executed between JCA, and the INS was a requirement contract and that the INS breached that contract by surreptitiously and illegally ordering services from contractors other than JCA; (2) the INS breached the letter contract by improperly and unreasonably failing to pay JCA's invoices; and (3) the INS breached the letter contract by its failure to act in good faith when it engaged in multiple and serious violations of procurement regulations—particularly regulations intended to protect SBA 8(a) contractors—for avoiding its contractual responsibilities to JCA.

The fundamental issue presented is whether the SBA, when serving as a party to a tripartite contract, will be found to have breached that contract where undisputed facts demonstrate that the SBA absolutely failed to fulfill its statutory and contractual duties owed to the primary party in privy with the SBA: The Section 8(a) contractor. JCA will demonstrate that, while the SBA was obligated to serve as an advisor and counselor to JCA and as a protective mediator between JCA and the INS, in this case, for a period of over three full months, unreasonably and inexplicably ignored JCA's multiple pleas for guidance and assistance. JCA will also show that, even after the SBA finally acted to respond to JCA's pleas, the SBA stood idly by while the INS, inter alia, attempted to impose unreasonable price terms upon JCA. Altogether, JCA will demonstrate that the SBA utterly failed to fulfill its most basic contractual duties to JCA.

II.   Statement of the Facts

A.   Background of J. Cooper & Associates

Mr. Joseph N. Cooper founded JCA in 1987 upon his departure from the federal government ("the government"), where he had served as the director of the Office of Federal Contract Compliance Programs ("OFCCP") from 1985 to 1987. As a former director of the OFCCP, Mr. Cooper was well known to the government contracting community and enjoyed an excellent reputation in that community.

As president of JCA, Mr. Cooper operated the company as a small, minority-owned business that provided a variety of consulting services, including public relations and advertising services. JCA's clients included Fortune 500 corporations such as Aetna Insurance, United Technologies, MCI, McDonnell Douglas, and Colgate Palmolive, as well as state governments and federal agencies. In 1992, JCA applied to the SBA to obtain certification to participate in the SBA Section 8(a) Program. In 1994, JCA had qualified for 8(a) certification. Also in 1994, JCA received the SBA's Minority Service Firm of the Year award. From its inception until it began performing under a letter contract with the INS, JCA had consistently earned a profit and maintained an excellent business reputation.

B. The Parties' Pre-Contract Discussions and the Award of the Letter Contract

In early 1995, the INS began efforts to select a contractor to perform an urgent INS requirement ("the requirement") for advertising and public relations services. The requirement involved the development and implementation of a marketing and advertising plan to improve and increase the recruitment of candidates for the Border Patrol and other offices of the INS. INS officials explored several options by which the requirement could be placed under contract as quickly as possible, including, inter alia, opening the procurement to full competition or limiting the procurement to the SBA 8(a) Program for Small and Disadvantaged Businesses ("SDB"). The INS acknowledged that one of the principal advantages offered by contracting with the Section 8(a) program was that a contract for the requirement could be awarded as early as July 1995, whereas if the requirement were opened to full competition, the contract could not be awarded until sometime in September 1995.

In or around mid-May 1995, the SBA Business Opportunity Specialist ("BOS") identified JCA as an 8(a) program SDB that possessed the qualifications to satisfy the requirement; and in June 1995, INS officials held meetings with JCA representatives regarding the requirement. During those June 1995 meetings, INS officials informed JCA that (1) the requirement would involve a number of varied and discrete tasks, such as placing advertisements in selected print and electronic media, preparing video tape presentations, and preparing a strategic plan to address the overall public relations and recruitment campaign; and (2) INS officials did not intend to contract separately with different contractors for each of the discrete tasks under the Contract but, instead, intended to have all of the public relations and advertising services performed by one contractor.

During the June 1995 meetings, INS officials informed JCA that the requirement would involve a possible multiyear, multimillion-dollar effort and stressed the urgency of the requirement. INS officials also informed JCA that it would need to have sufficient personnel and resources to handle a significant amount of immediate tasking from the INS and that JCA would need to hire additional personnel and to obtain facilities to ensure prompt performance of the anticipated tasks.

Also during the June 1995 meetings, INS officials informed JCA that the INS intended to award the contract for the requirement to JCA. At no time during any of the June 1995 meetings with JCA did the INS ever inform or indicate to JCA that the INS intended to use any contractor other than JCA to perform the INS requirement while JCA performed under the letter contract.

On June 30, 1995, the INS prepared a determination and findings memorandum, stating that the INS intended to process the requirement through the SBA as "an 8(a) requirement" and that the INS intended to enter into a letter contract to give JCA a binding commitment to begin work immediately on the INS requirement. JCA was the sole contractor for which the INS sought authorization to enter into a letter contract for the requirement. On July 7, 1995, the INS sent an "offering letter" to the SBA to offer the INS requirement to the Section 8(a) program. The offering letter estimated that the requirement would be valued at approximately $8 million over a five-year period. On or about July 7, 1995, the SBA accepted the entire INS requirement as a "set aside" requirement for both the SBA 8(a) program and JCA.

C. The Execution and Terms of the Letter Contract

Pursuant to Section 8(a) procedures, the INS entered into the Tripartite Letter Contract with the SBA and JCA. The INS supervisory contracting officer, Mr. Joseph M. Garforth, Jr., executed the letter contract on July 7, 1995, on behalf of the INS. Also on July 7, 1995, Mr. Joseph Cooper executed the letter contract on behalf of JCA. Mr. Shapleigh Drisko, the SBA contracting officer, executed the contract on behalf of the SBA on July 25, 1995. Pursuant to the provisions of the letter contract, the SBA served as the prime contractor to the INS, and JCA served as the subcontractor to the SBA.

The letter contract provided that the parties contemplated definitizing the contract as a "labor hours" indefinite delivery indefinite quantity ("IDIQ") contract. The terms of the letter contract itself, however, did not include the provision set forth at Federal Acquisition Regulation ("FAR") 52.216-22, "Indefinite Quantity" (the "IDIQ Provision") 16.505(e) (1994).[1] Ms. Michelle Wall, the INS contracting officer primarily responsible for administering the letter contract, understood that, although parties may have contemplated that the definitized contract would be an IDIQ contract, the letter contract was not an IDIQ contract.

Altogether, nothing in the letter contract provided or indicated that the INS intended to award any work relating to the requirement to any contractor other than JCA. Furthermore, the INS never informed or indicated to JCA that the INS intended to award any of the work under the requirement to any contractor other than JCA during JCA's performance of the letter contract.

D. SBA's Failure to Respond to JCA's Multiple Pleas for Assistance

From the award of the contract until late September 1995, JCA performed oral task orders as directed by INS personnel

---

[1] The FAR currently retains the same requirement at FAR 16.506(e) (1999).

and during this period JCA received only positive feedback on its performance under the contract. Toward the end of October 1995, however, JCA became concerned about its difficulties both with receiving payment from the INS and with satisfying the requests of the Defense Contract Auditing Agency ("DCAA") auditor who had been assigned to review JCA's proposal for the definitization of the contract.

In late September, JCA telephoned SBA officials to obtain guidance and assistance regarding the difficulties that JCA was having with the INS and the DCAA. However, no one from the SBA returned JCA's calls with any guidance or assistance. Next, on October 20, 1995, JCA sent a letter to the SBA BOS, in which JCA requested the SBA's assistance with the difficulties that JCA was experiencing under the contract. JCA informed the SBA BOS that (a) The INS's failure to issue task orders to JCA had presented a "serious financial problem" for JCA; (b) JCA had "geared up" for the contract by hiring additional personnel, buying additional equipment, obtaining additional office space, expanding its phone system, recruiting additional staff, and establishing an employee benefits plan, and because JCA did not have tasks to implement, JCA was "at risk financially"; (c) JCA had had trouble collecting payment for services rendered and that one invoice was already ninety days in arrears; and (d) JCA, "as a small business...[could not] withstand the level of delinquency that INS ha[d] imposed though failure to process invoices in a timely manner, or failure to release tasks in sufficient quantity to allow JCA to be successful." In the same letter, JCA also requested the SBA's assistance in arranging a tripartite meeting among JCA, SBA, and the INS to address the issues that had arisen under the contract. The SBA did not respond to the JCA's "October 20, 1995 letter" with any guidance or assistance until January 1996.

Beginning in early October 1995, JCA began sending the SBA BOS a series of courtesy copies of the correspondence that JCA was sending to the INS and to the DCAA regarding the problems that JCA was having with both receiving payment and the audit issues on the contract. The SBA failed to respond to any of this correspondence with any guidance or assistance until January 1996. In fact, JCA received no response of guidance and assistance from the SBA until sometime in January 1996—more than three months after JCA first requested assistance.

E. The INS's Refusal to Pay Invoices

During its June–July 1995 meeting and discussions with the INS, JCA informed the INS of the interim labor rates that JCA intended to charge under the letter contract, pending the final negotiation of rates. The INS did not object to the proposed rates, and JCA charged those interim rates on all invoices that JCA later submitted to the INS. Also, at no time prior to JCA's submission of its first invoice did the INS provide JCA with any guidance or instruction on the type of format or substantiation data that JCA should use or provide with its invoices.

On August 3, 1995, JCA submitted its first invoice ("Invoice No. 1") for services performed from July 12, 1995, to July 31, 1995. After receiving the invoice, the government requested that JCA revise the invoice to indicate each hour of labor charged under each labor category. On August 28, 1995, JCA responded by submitting a revised invoice that set forth a more detailed break-out of the hours and hourly rates for each of the persons who worked on the tasks. Invoice No. 1 billed the program director at a loaded rate of $167.86 per hour, the project lead at a loaded rate2 of $94.27 per hour, and the creative director/senior

---

2 A loaded rate is one that includes both direct and indirect labor charges in one, single rate.

writer at a loaded rate of $71.00 per hour. Soon thereafter, on September 11, 1995, JCA submitted its second invoice ("Invoice No. 2") to the INS requesting payment in amount of $74,545 for services performed during the period August 1–31, 1995.

By late September 1995, JCA had not received any payment from the INS. At this time, JCA notified the INS both that, as a small company, JCA could not afford to carry two invoices for sixty days without collecting some form of interest on the invoices and that the INS's failure to pay JCA was putting JCA's ability to perform in jeopardy. On October 5, 1995, JCA submitted its third invoice ("Invoice No. 3"), which billed for $108,528.76 in services and covered the performance period from September 1–30, 1995. On the same date, JCA once again requested that the INS pay JCA's invoices promptly, because JCA was having difficulties continuing to perform without receiving prompt payment from the INS.

It was not until October 20, 1995, that the INS made its first payment to JCA; the INS paid JCA Invoice No. 1 in full. On November 13, 1995, JCA submitted its fourth invoice ("Invoice No. 4") to the INS; Invoice No. 4 sought reimbursement for $67,501.43 for services performed during the period from October 1–31, 1995.

On November 22, 1995, the INS contracting officer requested for the first time that the DCAA review Invoices Nos. 2 and 3. On or about December 12, 1995, the INS paid JCA only $47,667.31 of the $74,545.00 of the amounts invoiced under Invoice No. 2 and only $67,942.82 of the $108,528.76 of the amounts invoiced under Invoice No. 3, resulting in a total payment of $115,610.13 instead of the $183,073.76 as invoiced.

On or about February 5, 1996, the DCAA completed its audit of Invoice No. 4. Thereafter, on or about March 19, 1995, the INS paid only $34,327.07 of the $67,501.43 that had been invoiced under Invoice No. 4. Moreover, the INS for the first time unilaterally reduced the individual labor rates charged for JCA's employees under Invoice No. 4. Specifically, the INS reduced the program director rate from $167.86 to $55.03, reduced the project lead rate from $94.27 to $61.81 per hour, and reduced the creative director/senior writer rate from $71.00 to $46.56 per hour. As of March 19, 1996, the INS informed JCA that, based on the DCAA's audits, JCA was entitled to no more than the amounts that the INS had already paid under Invoices Nos. 1 through 4.

On or about September 16, 1996, the DCAA issued a second audit report, prepared by a different auditor, on JCA's Invoices, Nos. 1–4. When the DCAA conducted this "second" audit report, JCA provided the DCAA the very same data that JCA had earlier provided to the DCAA to support its first audits of JCA Invoices 1–4, when the DCAA originally audited those invoices in late 1995 and early 1996.

According to the September 16, 1996, audit, the DCAA determined that JCA was entitled to payment of an additional $49,936.22 for the amounts invoiced under Invoices 1–4. Moreover, on this second audit, the DCAA declined to reduce the individual loaded labor rates charged by JCA's employees under Invoice No. 4.

It was not until November 18, 1996, that the INS decided that it would pay JCA an additional $49,936.22 for services rendered under JCA's Invoices 1–4. Prior to this payment, the INS had maintained that it had received less than $231,000 in services from JCA. Thus, only by this belated payment was the INS able to state that it had "ordered" from JCA services valued in excess of $250,000.

F. INS's Unreasonable Refusal to Issue Task Orders to JCA

When the INS began issuing task orders to JCA on or about July 12, 1995, the urgency of the requirement led the INS to issue oral, rather than written, task orders. The INS continued to issue all oral task orders to JCA throughout July, August, and early September 1995. During the period from July 12 through September 21, 1995, no one from the INS ever indicated to JCA that anyone at the INS had experienced problems with JCA's performance of the INS's oral task orders.

In or about mid-September 1995, the INS program office hired Ms. Eleanor Miller and assigned her to work with the JCA contract. Soon after she arrived at the INS, Ms. Miller attended a meeting during which INS officials discussed the JCA contract. Ms. Miller recorded her understanding at that meeting that the INS officials at that time wanted or had "nothing in writing." The meeting record indicated that the INS officials at that time intended to "do [a] delivery order to spend [the] rest of [the] money" that was then available on the contract. Nevertheless, beginning on or about September 21, 1995, Ms. Miller began preparing a series of memoranda that were highly critical of JCA's performance on the contract and explored the INS's options to end its relationship with JCA.

First, on or about September 21, 1995, Ms. Miller prepared a memorandum that excoriated the draft of the strategic plan that had been prepared by JCA. In the same September 21, 1995, memorandum, Ms. Miller sought the contracting office's advice as to when "can we end the relationship with one firm and begin working with another firm." Ms. Miller also inquired whether the INS could "change the [contract's] statement of work" and suggested that "perhaps ad placement should be separated out from the larger recruitment strategy contract." Ms. Miller also queried the contracting office personnel as to whether the INS program office could "have a BPA [Blanket Purchase Agreement, or "BPA"] for quick turnaround items" like ad placement and article writing.

In a memorandum dated October 3, 1995, Ms. Miller outlined her plan to: "work with the [INS contracting officer] to prepare a memo to [the] contractor advising [the] contractor that...no further work...based on any previous discussion, should continue at this time due to the cost [sic] limitations imposed upon INS by the Letter Contract." In the same memorandum, Ms. Miller also outlined her plan to "let [a] small purchase contract for [a] list of 'target audience' publications and conferences for FY 96." As of early October 1995, the INS had ceased to issue any more task orders to JCA.

On or about October 13, 1995, Ms. Miller was designated as the contracting officer's technical representative ("COTR") on the letter contract. During Ms. Miller's tenure as COTR of the contract, INS contracting office personnel observed friction between Ms. Miller and Mr. Cooper. Even before she was designated as the COTR, Ms. Miller had expressed that her beliefs regarding JCA's honesty and integrity were "flavoring her opinions" of JCA. Later, an INS contracting official remarked that Ms. Miller had allowed the "business and the personal to cross" , in her dealings with JCA. Moreover, the contracting official specifically determined that Ms. Miller had an "inability to work professionally with [JCA]." The contracting official observed that "prior to the hiring of [Ms. Miller] the Government had no concerns over [JCA's] performance problems."

On or about December 1, 1995, Mr. Joseph Garforth, the supervisory contracting officer on the JCA contract, advised Ms. Wall to write a letter to JCA regarding JCA's alleged "poor performance" based primarily upon the matters raised in the memorandum that Ms. Miller had prepared on or about September 21, 1995. The INS, however, never prepared or issued any letter or other written guidance, comment, or notice whatsoever to JCA regarding its alleged poor performance on the contract. In fact, the INS supervisory contracting officer for the contract, Mr. Garforth, testified that the INS contracting office had refused to issue any letter to JCA regarding its alleged poor performance, because the INS program office personnel, including Ms. Miller, had failed to "back up" their allegations of JCA's poor performance.

In early to mid-October 1995, JCA asked the INS contracting officials whether the INS intended to issue any other task orders to JCA. On or about October 13, 1995, Ms. Wall and Ms. Greene responded by assuring JCA that the INS intended to issue additional task orders to JCA "as soon as practicable." Ms. Wall also informed JCA that the INS also intended to prepare an "umbrella" task order to cover all of the meetings and conferences relating to the contract that JCA had been required to attend.

When JCA still had not received any task orders by late October 1995, JCA again asked Ms. Wall when the promised task orders would be issued. Ms. Wall again assured JCA that the INS still intended to issue task orders to JCA. Moreover, throughout the period from late October 1995 until mid-March 1996, JCA repeatedly asked the INS if it intended to issue further task orders to JCA. On each occasion, the INS assured JCA that the INS did intend to issue more task orders.

Meanwhile, instead of issuing task orders to JCA, the INS, as of October 31, 1995, had begun to order services for the requirement under an INS BPA with the first of many contractors other than JCA. During the period from October 31, 1995, through May 16, 1996, the INS ordered tens, if not hundreds, of thousands of dollars in services for the requirement from firms other than JCA, including non-Section 8(a) firms. However, at no time during JCA's performance of the letter contract did the INS inform JCA that the INS was satisfying its requirement through contractors other than JCA.

On or about March 19, 1996, the INS requested that JCA prepare a proposal to perform a task order, involving the development of both black-and-white and full-color ads for the U.S. Border Patrol ("Task Order No. 2"). INS contracting office representatives assured JCA that the INS would issue the task order to JCA, if the INS approved JCA's proposal. This proposed task order was critical to JCA, because it represented JCA's final chance to continue to perform the contract.

Prior to JCA's submission of its proposal to perform Task Order No. 2, an INS contracting office representative specifically observed that the COTR had not provided the contracting office with (1) any government price estimate from which to negotiate or (2) any funded requisition for the task, which would indicate what the program office expected the task to cost. The contracting official went on to state that she would be "professionally and personally reluctant to allow [the INS] to become completely arbitrary in our decision process on this matter [the evaluation of JCA's proposal]."

On April 4, 1996, JCA submitted a proposal to perform Task Order No. 2 for a price of $58,024.76, including a 10 percent profit or fee. Upon receipt of JCA's price proposal for Task Order No. 2 on April 17, 1996, Ms. Miller complained that the order should not be issued to JCA, because JCA's proposed price was "outrageous." Ms. Miller based her statement on the fact that she had received an informal, "rough estimate" offer of $5,667.00 from a JCA competitor to perform the task.

During late April and early May 1996, the INS proceeded to conduct price negotiations with JCA over the price it had proposed for Task Order No. 2. During the negotiations, JCA explained to the INS that its price position for the performance of Task Order No. 2 was so low as to be "far off base." JCA explained that it could not reasonably perform Task Order No. 2 for any amount significantly less than the approximately $58,000 price that it had originally proposed.

In the end, the INS refused to issue Task Order No. 2 to JCA, because JCA refused to significantly reduce its proposed price to perform the task order. Later, the INS obtained an independent government estimate for the cost to perform Task Order No. 2. The independent estimate found that Task Order No. 2 should have cost "$75K versus the $57K quoted by [JCA]."

The SBA contracting officer, Mr. Drisko, testified that the SBA would ask an agency to provide the basis for an estimate of the fair market price of the goods or services that an SBA contractor was to provide to the INS in the event that the cost or price of the item became a major issue under the SBA contract. The SBA was informed of the negotiations over Task Order No. 2 and knew about the INS's belief that JCA's proposed price was excessively high. The SBA also knew that this proposed task order was critical to JCA's continued performance of the contract. The SBA, however, made no attempt to obtain from the INS any data relating to the INS's basis for the price it attempted to negotiate with JCA.

Based upon the INS officials' repeated assurances that they intended to issue more task orders to JCA, JCA continued to coordinate with INS officials to perform the letter contract and to work toward its definitization from early October 1995 until May 1996. These matters included, inter alia, attending meetings with INS, DCAA and, later, SBA officials regarding the alleged issues with JCA's performance on the contract; hiring several consultants to make numerous revisions to JCA's proposal for the definitization of the contract; preparing technical and price proposals for task orders; and meeting and corresponding with the DCAA officials regarding alleged issues with the definitization proposal and JCA's invoices.

JCA continued its efforts to perform on the matters relating to the contract until early May 1996, when JCA began to learn of credible rumors that the INS had actually issued task orders to another contractor to perform tasks under the INS requirement. Upon learning of the rumors, JCA, in early May 1996, contacted the INS and suggested that the INS terminate the letter contract because JCA had become "convinced that [the INS was] interested in doing business with a firm other than [JCA]."

On or about May 16, 1996, the INS proposed to the SBA that it should agree to allow the letter contract to "lapse" and that the SBA should request the contractor to prepare a proposal for costs incurred in the performance of the contract.

Also on May 16, 1996, the INS provided its first written notice to the SBA that the INS intended to procure services for the requirement from non-8(a) firms. The INS contracting officer who provided the notice to the SBA testified to his under-standing that the INS had an obligation to notify the SBA when the INS had decided to satisfy its requirement by us-ing non-Section 8(a) contractors.

On June 26, 1996, JCA submitted a termination settlement claim ("Claim") to the INS contracting officer. On December 9, 1996, the INS issued a final decision (the "Final Decision") through its contracting officer, denying JCA's claim. On December 8, 1997, JCA appealed the INS's Final Decision de-nying the claim to the United States Court of Federal Claims ("CFC"); the appeal was docketed under CFC No. 97-839C.

It was extremely costly for JCA to continue to attempt to perform the letter contract until May 1996, when JCA had not received any new task orders since late September 1995, and had not received full payment of its services as invoiced. Moreover, JCA expended significant sums from late October 1995 to May 1996 to consultants to address DCAA's alleged issues with JCA's proposal and invoices. These costs not only exhausted JCA's corporate reserves but also exhausted Mr. Cooper's personal sources of income and credit. As a direct result of this exhaustion of personal and corporate funds, Mr. Cooper was forced to terminate all business activities of JCA. Thus, in mid-1997, JCA was no longer a going concern. Also, as of March 1997, Mr. Cooper was forced to declare personal bankruptcy to ameliorate the debt that he had accumulated as a direct result of the ruin of JCA.

SUMMARY OF ARGUMENT

As a matter of law, the government breached its letter contract with JCA. The INS, through the contract, obligated itself to purchase all of its advertising needs relating to a specific requirement from JCA. The contract was a requirements-type contract because of the government's promises of exclusivity and the manner the contract was written. Because it is undisputed that it ordered advertising services from contractors other than JCA, the INS breached the contract.

The government owed a duty of cooperation to JCA during contract performance. The government breached its duty to not do anything to hinder JCA's performance by depriving JCA of work under the contract and by failing to deal professionally with JCA. The INS evaded its contract obligations in part through violations of procurement regulations, such as use of BPAs structured to avoid small purchase thresholds. The INS's actions in violation of federal procurement law are a breach of the government's contract. Additionally, the government had a basic obligation to timely pay JCA for its performance. The government's failure to do so was a breach of the contract.

Also as a matter of law, the SBA's failure to act on JCA's behalf was a breach of the SBA's obligations imposed by statute, regulation, and the contract. During JCA's performance under the contract, JCA repeatedly requested the SBA's assistance—which the SBA is statutorily required to provide—including technical and managerial aid, intervention with the government agency, and fair pricing of the contract. The SBA failed to render assistance to JCA, regarding audit requirements as well as fair price negotiations with the INS. The SBA's failures violated applicable statutes and regulations and breached its contractual duty to cooperate with JCA.

ARGUMENT

I. The INS Breached the Contract by Failing to Fulfill Its Contractual Duties to JCA

The INS, SBA, and JCA were parties to the tripartite letter contract. The full record is replete with evidence of multiple breaches by the INS of its contract with JCA; however, for the purposes of this motion, plaintiff will focus only upon the undisputed facts demonstrating that the INS breached the contract by (1) failing to order advertising services for its requirement solely from JCA; (2) failing to fulfill its obligation to perform the contract in good faith by evading its bargain with JCA and accomplishing this evasion through multiple violations of federal procurement law; and ; (3) failing to pay JCA for services performed under the contract.

A. The INS Breached the Contract by Ordering Advertising Services Identified in the Requirement from Contractors Other Than JCA

When the government diverts its business away from a party with whom it has executed a requirements contract, the diversion constitutes a breach of contract. (See *Torncello*

v. *United States*, 231 Ct. Cl. 20, 48, 681 F.2d 756, 772 (Ct. Cl. 1982); diversion of requirements was a breach of contract by the government.) As plaintiff will demonstrate herein, JCA's letter contract was a requirements contract, and the INS breached this contract by procuring from other contractors tens, perhaps hundreds, of thousands of dollars of the services during the period of JCA's performance of the letter contract.

1. The Letter Contract Is a Requirements Contract.

Whether or not a contract is a requirements-type contract is a question of law. (See *Crown Laundry & Dry Cleaners, Inc. v, United States*, 29 Fed. Cl. 506, 515 (1993); contract determined to be a requirements contract based on intention of the contracting parties.) In making its determination, the court will look at the text of the contract, as well as the facts and circumstances surrounding the formation of the contract at issue. (See *Torncello*, 231 Ct. Cl. at 28-29, 681 F.2d at 761-762.) The primary distinguishing test of a requirements contract is "whether it is implicit in [the contract] terms, or in the circumstances surrounding the formation of the contract, that the [government] promised to give all of its work authorizations to [plaintiff] or whether the [government] could use other contractors, too" (*Torncello*, 231 Ct. Cl. at 28, 681 F.2d at 761).

Applying this standard to the undisputed facts of JCA's contract with the INS, the tripartite letter contract was a requirements contract, because the text of the contract, as well as the circumstances of contract formation, confirm that the INS intended to award all of its advertising requirements to JCA during JCA's performance of the letter contract. (See *Ceredo Mortuary Chapel v. United States*, 29

Fed. Cl. 346, 351 (1993); agreement revealed several "hall-marks" of a requirements contract.)

Prior to the execution of the letter contract, high-level INS officials expressly informed JCA that, although the contract would require performance of a number of varied and discrete tasks, the INS intended to have one contractor perform all of these tasks. Furthermore, pursuant to the determination and findings memorandum executed on June 30, 1995, JCA was the sole contractor for which the INS sought authorization to issue a binding commitment to work under a letter contract for the INS's requirement. The INS never informed or indicated to JCA that the INS intended to award any of the work under the requirement to any contractor other than JCA during the performance of the initial letter contract, and JCA never understood that INS intended to have any contractor other than JCA perform the requirement while JCA performed under the letter contract.

Regarding the letter contract as executed, no term of the contract provided or indicated that the INS intended to award any work relating to the requirement to any contractor other than JCA prior to definitization of the letter contract. The letter contract did not include the provision at FAR 52.216-22, "Indefinite Quantity" specified by then-applicable FAR provision 16.505(e). (See FAR 16.505(e) (1994).) Instead, the contract merely provided that the parties contemplated definitizing the contract as an indefinite delivery, indefinite quantity ("IDIQ") contract. The INS contracting officer responsible for administering the letter contract acknowledged her understanding that, although the parties may have contemplated that the contract would be definitized as an IDIQ contract, the letter contract itself was not an IDIQ contract.

It is uncontested that the government drafted the letter contract. If the government did not intend to form an exclusive contract, it was incumbent upon the government to state in the contract, by "extensive and visible treatment," that it was not exclusive. (*Ceredo*, 29 Fed. Cl. at 352.) Every fact indicates that the INS did not express any intent other than that the letter contract was an exclusive one. The government's failure to include a nonexclusive provision must be construed against it. Moreover, if a contract is susceptible of interpretation as either an IDIQ or requirements contract, the court should "uphold it as of the requirements type." (See A-Transport Northwest Co., Inc., 27 Fed. Cl. 206, 214 (1992), quoting *Ralph Constr., Inc. v. United States*, 4 Cl. Ct. 727, 732 (1984), aff'd, 36 F.3d 1576 (Fed. Cir. 1994).) Accordingly, the contract should be interpreted as a requirements-type contract.

2. The INS Procured Advertising Services Identified in the Requirement from Contractors Other Than JCA

It is undisputed that the INS ordered services for the requirement from contractors other than JCA. It is also undisputed that the INS began ordering the services while JCA's undefinitized letter contract remained fully in force. By ordering services for the requirement from contractors other than JCA, the INS acted in contravention of the letter contract, which, as has already been demonstrated, was a requirements contract. (See *Laboratory for Electronics, Inc.*, ASBCA No. 13019, 69-2 BCA ¶ 7945, at 36,944; parties bound by content of undefinitized letter contract,) Given these facts, the INS breached the letter contract. (See, e.g., *Torncello*, 231 Ct. Cl. at 28, 681 F.2d at 671.)

B. The INS Breached the Contract by Failing to Cooperate with JCA and by Acting in Violation of Federal Procurement Law

The INS also breached the contract through illegally evading its contractual responsibilities to JCA. The undisputed facts show that the INS failed to cooperate with JCA and abused and violated the FAR's simplified acquisition procedures to accomplish its plan of evasion—using BPAs to order services from non-SBA contractors to avoid the INS's obligations to JCA. Moreover, the record shows that the INS failed to provide the requisite notice to the SBA when the INS acted to procure services for the requirement from non-Section 8(a) contractors.

The government has a fundamental duty in any contract to comport with "standards of good faith and fair dealing" (*Malone v. United States*, 849 F.2d 1441, 1446 (Fed. Cir.) (quoting Restatement (Second) of Contracts § 241(e) (1981)), modified on other grounds, 857 F.2d 787 (Fed. Cir. 1988)). Resort to "'subterfuges and evasions violate the obligation of good faith,' as does lack of diligence and interference with or failure to cooperate in the other party's performance." Id.(quoting Restatement (Second) of Contracts § 205 comment d (1981)). The undisputed record demonstrates that the INS violated its obligations to comport with standards of good faith and fair dealing by its evasions of its contractual obligations to JCA through a scheme of FAR violations.

1. The INS Failed to Cooperate with JCA

The government's duty of fair dealing means that the government must cooperate with the contractor and not do anything to hinder its performance. (See, e.g., *Celeron Gathering Corp. v. United States*, 34 Fed. Cl. 745, 752 (1996); *Smith v. United States*, 34 Fed. Cl. 313, 321 (1995), appeal dismissed, 91 F.3d 165 (1996); *O'Neill v. United States*, 231 Ct. Cl. 823, 825 (1982).) The undisputed record shows that the INS maladministered the letter contract by allowing program office representatives to issue verbal—and, often, conflicting—task orders to JCA. The undisputed record also shows that, while JCA was attempting to perform the letter contract, certain INS program office representatives began unjustifiably to make every effort to bring the JCA contract to an end. These INS officials, particularly the COTR, attempted to "paper the file" with adverse memoranda regarding JCA's alleged "performance problems." However, the program office's attempt to convince the INS contracting officer to issue written notice to JCA of its alleged "poor performance" failed, because the INS contracting office flatly refused to acquiesce to this adverse action against JCA. Specifically, the contracting officer refused to issue the adverse notice to JCA, because the INS program office had failed to "back up" its allegations of performance problems by JCA.

As the INS program office representatives continued their baseless efforts to rid themselves of JCA, it became clear that they had allowed the lines between personal feelings and business relations to cross. Apparently unable and unwilling to deal fairly, honestly, and openly with JCA, the INS undertook to undermine and avoid its contract with JCA. Such actions are not permissible. (Cf. *Darwin Constr. Co. v. United States*, 811 F.2d 593, 595 (Fed. Cir. 1987), actions taken solely to "rid" a government agency of dealing with contractor not allowed.) As discussed infra, the INS began ordering services for the requirement from contractors other than JCA. Moreover, it is undisputed that the INS ordered those services through BPAs and never notified JCA of these orders. The INS's conduct of concealing its use of the BPAs from JCA deprived JCA of the ability to timely protest those activities and caused JCA to continue performing well beyond the period after the INS had effectively ended the contract. It would be unconscionable to allow the INS to avoid the consequences of its illegal activities just because it succeeded in hiding them from JCA. (See *Malone*, 849 F. 2d at 1446.)

The INS program office's failure to cooperate with JCA came to a head during the negotiations over Task Order No. 2, from March 1996 through May 1996. The program office indicated it was giving JCA one "last chance" to perform under the letter contract, but frustrated JCA's attempt to do so. The program office entered negotiations without a formal price estimate or a funded requisition estimating the cost of performing the task. When JCA submitted a proposal priced at $58,024.76, the INS COTR obtained "informal" offers from other companies. There were no guarantees as to the accuracy, reliability, or relevance of such quotes. The COTR's fundamental misunderstanding of contract requirements and unfairness to JCA is shown by the fact that an independent government entity priced the work required under Task Order No. 2 at $75,000.

2. The INS Violated Federal Procurement Laws to Evade Its Contract with JCA

Not only did the INS act in bad faith by subverting its contract with JCA, it also broke the law in doing so. It is well established that the FAR has the force of law. (See *Davies Precision Mach., Inc. v. United States*, 35 Fed. Cl. 651, 657 (1996), FAR had the "force and effect of law"; cf. *Mapco Alaska Petroleum, Inc. v. United States*, 27 Fed. Cl. 405, 407–08 (1992), "applicable provisions of the [Federal Acquisition Regulations] are incorporated into every federal government procurement contract and have the same effect as if they were set forth in the contract itself.") Therefore, to the extent that the INS used means and methods contrary to applicable regulations as part of its scheme to rid itself of JCA, the INS breached its contract with JCA.[3] (See *Allenfield Assocs. v. United States*, 40 Fed. Cl.471,482 (1998), "applicable laws are binding on parties to a contract.") Whether JCA's contract with the INS was a requirements contract or an IDIQ contract, the use of improper conduct to avoid contractual obligations is a breach of contract. (Cf. *Malone*, 849 F. 2d at 1445-46.)

a. The INS Violated the FAR by Using BPAs to Order Services for the Requirement

First, the INS violated the FAR provisions governing simplified acquisition procedures by awarding contracts to firms other than JCA through BPAs. In pertinent part, the FAR provides that simplified acquisition procedures, which include the use of BPAs, cannot be used if the government's acquisition of supplies or services is initially expected to exceed the simplified acquisition threshold. (See FAR 13.101 (1995); FAR 13.103(c) (1995).) The FAR also forbids breaking a requirement down into smaller requirements to skirt the simplified acquisition threshold. At the time of the letter contract, the simplified acquisition threshold was $100,000. (See FAR 13.101 (1995).) It is undisputed that the value of the INS requirement under which JCA performed, however, was estimated to total $8 million. Furthermore, the undisputed facts confirm that, regardless of the fact that the estimated value of the INS requirement unquestionably exceeded the

---

3 See *Wells Fargo Bank, N.A. v. United States*, 33 Fed. Cl. 233 (1995), rev'd in part on other grounds, 88 F. 3d 1012 (Fed. Cir. 1996), cert. denied, 520 U.S. 1116 (1997); *AT&T Technologies, Inc. v. United States*, 18 Cl. Ct. 315 (1989); Johnson & Son Erectors Co., ASBCA Nos. 23689, 24564, 81-1 BCA ¶ 14,880 at 73,581 ("the Government's supposed violation of the procurement regulations appears to be one which, if established, would amount to a breach of contract and, perhaps, call for recission or reformation action."); Doris A. Lahage, GSBCA No. 7321, 84-2 BCA ¶ 17,498 at 87,154 ("the Government's failure was a breach of its duty as prescribed by the regulations"); Adams Mfg. Co., GSBCA No. 5747, 82-1 BCA ¶ 15,740 at 77,889 ("When the Government decided not to follow those regulations in determining its requirements, it committed a breach of its contractual obligation to do so").

applicable simplified acquisition procedure threshold, the INS nevertheless proceeded to use BPAs to order tens and perhaps hundreds of thousands of dollars' worth of services satisfy the requirement. Thus, there is no doubt that this action by the INS flatly violated the regulations governing FAR simplified acquisition procedures.[4]

b. The INS Violated the FAR by Its Failure to Notify the SBA that the INS Had Ordered Services for the Requirement from Non-8(a) Contractors

Second, the INS violated the FAR provisions mandating that the INS provide notice to the SBA once the INS had determined to satisfy its requirement with non-Section 8(a) concerns. The FAR mandates that agencies must provide written notice to the SBA when an agency decides to withdraw or modify its small business set-aside determination. (See FAR 19.506(c) (1995).) As demonstrated below, the INS violated this requirement by failing to notify the SBA when the INS of its decision to order services for its requirement from non-8a concerns

The INS determination and finding for authorization to contract for the requirement provided that the INS intended to procure the entire requirement from the SBA Section 8(a) program. The INS offered the entire requirement to the SBA Section 8(a) program, and the SBA accepted the entire requirement as a set-aside procurement for the Section 8(a)

---

4 The INS conduct violated both the letter and the spirit of the FAR regulations governing simplified acquisition procedures. One of the purposes of simplified acquisition procedures is to "[i]mprove opportunities for small business and small disadvantaged business concerns to obtain a fair proportion of Government contracts" (FAR 13.102(b) (1995)). In its scheme to avoid JCA, however, the INS used the simplified acquisition procedures to do just the opposite—to deny opportunities to a Section 8(a) business. Furthermore, the INS's use of BPAs violates the FAR's stated purpose of protecting small business set-asides. FAR 13.204(c) (1995) states that "the existence of a BPA does not justify purchasing from only one source or avoiding small business set-asides." (Emphasis added).

program. Altogether, the undisputed facts confirm that the INS requirement was set aside entirely for the Section 8(a) program.

At least as early as March 13, 1996, the INS had begun ordering advertising services for its requirement through the award of task orders under a BPA with the firm J. Walter Thompson. As of March 13, 1996, the firm J. Walter Thompson was not a Section 8(a) concern. The INS COTR who awarded the task orders for the requirement under the BPAs understood that J. Walter Thompson was not a Section 8(a) concern.

In a letter dated May 16, 1996, the INS provided its first written notice to the SBA regarding the INS's intention to procure services for its requirement from non-Section 8(a) concerns. In this same letter, the contracting officer confirmed his belief the INS was obligated to notify the SBA when the INS decided to satisfy the requirement through non-Section 8(a) contractors.

The INS's act of awarding BPAs and small purchase orders to non-8(a) contractors such as J. Walter Thompson violated FAR 13.204(a) (1995). This violation of regulations designed to protect small business concerns is the type of conduct that breaches the implied contractual duty of good faith and fair dealing. (See *Dubinsky v. United States*, 43 Fed. Cl. 243, 260 (1999); cf. *Malone*, 849 F. 2d at 1445–46.)

Altogether, the undisputed facts show that the INS requirement was set aside for the Section 8(a) program and that the INS failed to provide written notice to the SBA of the INS's decision in March 1996 to use non-Section 8(a) concerns to satisfy the INS requirement. On these facts, the INS clearly violated the mandate of FAR 19.506(c) (1995). Moreover, this INS violation of FAR 19.506(c) and the INS's multiple violations of the FAR provisions governing simplified acquisition procedures were integral parts of the INS's over-all conduct to rid itself of JCA and to evade its contractual duties to JCA. This INS conduct was improper and illegal and constituted a breach of contract. (Cf. *Malone*, 849 F. 2d at 1445–46.)

C. The INS Breached the Contract by Its Prolonged Failure to Pay JCA

1. The Government Had a Contractual Duty to Pay JCA.

One of the government's basic obligations in a contract for products or services is to timely pay the party providing such products or services, and the failure to make timely payment is a breach of the government's "contractual obligation." (See, e.g., TEM Associates, Inc., DOT BCA No. 2024, 89-1 BCA 21,266, at 107,221; *Northern Helex Co. v. United States*, 197 Ct. Cl. 118, 124, 455 F. 2d 546, 548 (Ct. Cl. 1972).) As shown below, the government clearly failed to timely pay JCA for services performed under the contract, thereby breaching the contract.

2. The Government Failed to Pay JCA

Every invoice submitted by JCA to INS for services performed under the letter contract contained (a) JCA's name; (b) the invoice date; (c) the contract number; (d) description, quantity, unit of measurement, unit price and extended price of the services performed; and (e) JCA's name and address. Thus, JCA's invoices were prepared in the form required by FAR 32.905(e) (1995).

The government, however, failed to make payment within thirty days of the first invoice, and the extent of the government's failure to make timely payment grew with nearly every passing invoice. The government did not pay JCA's first invoice for nearly two months, and then did not attempt to pay the second for nearly three months after that. There was also a two-month gap in the government's partial payment of Invoice No. 3. The INS did not attempt to pay JCA's Invoice No. 4 until March 19, 1996—a gap of over four months. Finally, the INS did not make its final payment for services performed by JCA solely under Invoices 1–4 until November 18, 1996—more than a year after JCA had submitted the first of those invoices.

As JCA repeatedly notified the government, the INS's slow payment of the invoices put a significant strain on JCA's operations and imperiled its stability. Despite JCA's communication of the urgent need for payment, the government repeatedly delayed payment of JCA's invoices for prolonged periods of time—and when it paid, it did so only partially. Such failure to make timely payment is a breach of contract. (See, e.g., *Northern Helex*, 197 Ct. Cl. at 124, 455 F. 2d at 548; *Brooklyn & Queens Screen Mfg. Co. v. United States*, 97 Ct. Cl. 532, 543 (1942), failure to pay monthly estimate of approximately $2,250 for work performed in September constituted breach by October; *Suburban Contracting Co. v. United States*, 76 Ct. Cls. 533, 536 (1932), one month's negligent delay in paying voucher justified rescinding contract.) The government's failure to make payment was particularly egregious, as it occurred in the context of an 8(a) program contract. (See Nexus Constr. Co., ASBCA No. 31070, 92-2 BCA 24,923; withholding of progress payments for several months was a breach of an 8(a) contract.)

1. The Government Unilaterally Reduced Agreed-upon Labor Rates

Not only did the government make payments late, it also unjustifiably sought to shortchange JCA by unilaterally reducing the labor rates it had previously agreed upon. During the June 1995 meetings, JCA had discussed with INS officials the interim labor rates that JCA intended to apply to the letter contract, and the INS never objected to those proposed rates. Moreover, the INS did not object to the labor rates as set forth in all of JCA's invoices and in fact paid the rates as invoiced by JCA under the first three invoices.

On March 19, 1996, however, the INS for the first time unilaterally reduced the individual labor rates charged for JCA's employees under Invoice No. 4. Specifically, the INS reduced the program director per-hour loaded rate from $167.86 to $55.03, reduced the project lead per-hour loaded rate from $94.27 to $61.81, and reduced the creative director/senior writer per-hour loaded rate from $71.00 to $46.56. The INS did not repay JCA for this unilateral wage rate reduction until November 1996, over seven months after JCA had submitted Invoice No. 4 to the INS. In all, this unilateral reduction of JCA's labor rates constituted another unreasonable and prolonged failure by the INS fulfill its obligation to pay JCA; therefore, this failure constituted a breach of contract. (See, e.g., Restatement (Second) of Contracts § 235 (1981), Northern Helex, 197 Ct. Cl. at 124, 455 F. 2d at 548.)

II. The SBA Breached Its Contract with JCA by Failing to Fulfill the SBA's Contractual Duties to JCA

The SBA, JCA's other party to the tripartite letter contract, failed to meet its obligation to JCA, as required by the contract, statute, and regulation. As plaintiff will demonstrate, the SBA breached the contract by the SBA's failure to (1) fulfill the contractual duties owed to JCA, as those duties are expressly imposed upon the SBA by statute, regulation, and agency procedure; and (2) fulfill the contractual duties owed to JCA, as those duties are implied and imposed under all common-law contracts.

A. The SBA Breached its Contractual Duties to JCA by Failing to Fulfill Duties Expressly Imposed by Its Enabling Statute and Implementing Regulations

The SBA's enabling statute, regulations, and SOP expressly impose upon the SBA duties that it must fulfill in favor of Section 8(a) concerns. These duties include, inter alia, (1) providing technical and managerial aids and counseling and assistance to SBA 8(a) concerns and acting as an advocate and protecting the interest of 8(a) concerns and (2) making every effort to ensure that 8(a) concerns are offered contracts at a "fair market price" and contracts that will enable the 8(a) concern to make a "reasonable profit." As shown below, however, the SBA failed to fulfill any of these duties owed to JCA, thereby breaching its contract with JCA.

1. The SBA Breached the Contract by Failing to Aid and Assist JCA and Failing to Protect JCA's Interests in Its Dealings with the INS

The SBA's enabling statute imposes upon the SBA the duty to provide technical and managerial assistance to Section 8(a) concerns such as JCA as follows:

It shall...be the duty of the [SBA] and it is empowered, whenever it determines such action is necessary... *to provide technical* and managerial aids to small business concerns, by advising and counseling on matters in connection with Government procurement and property disposal and on policies, principles, and practices of good management, including but not limited to cost accounting. (15 U.S.C. § 637(b) (1) (A) (1994), emphasis added)

The same statute also imposes upon the SBA the duty to ensure that 8(a) concerns receive "fair and reasonable treatment" from federal agencies (such as the INS) with which the SBA and the Section 8(a) concern contract:

It shall also be the duty of the [SBA] and it is empowered, whenever it determines such action is necessary...to consult and cooperate with all Government agencies for the purpose of ensuring that small-business concerns receive fair and reasonable treatment from such agencies. (15 U.S.C. § 637(b)(1)(1994), emphasis added)

These duties are further underscored in the SBA's implementing regulations, particularly with regard to Section 8(a) concerns.[5]

For example, the SBA regulations provide that it has a duty to aid, counsel, assist, and protect the interests of Section 8(a) concerns in their dealings with federal agencies (13 C.F.R. § 101.1 (1995); see also 15 U.S.C. § 631 (1994)). As explained in *A & S Council Oil Co. v. Saiki*, Section 8(a) concerns such as JCA have a justifiable expectation that they can rely on the SBA for some form of assistance when faced with difficulties dealing with a procurement agency under a tripartite contract: "[T]he SBA's role in the 8(a) program is

---

5 Relevant SBA implementing regulations are found at 13 C.F.R. Part 101 ("Administration") and 13 C.F.R. Part 124 (Section 8(a) implementing regulations). 13 C.F.R. § 124.1 (1995) ("Scope of regulations") states that "[t]hese regulations [Part 124] implement section] 8(a)...of the Small Business Act [15 U.S.C. § 637(a)]."

one of a mediator, a fiduciary of sorts, and a guarantor.... With the SBA in the middle, *section 8(a) firms have justifiably come to rely on the SBA to assist with the problems these firms face"* (799 F. Supp. 1221, 1235 (D.D.C. 1992), emphasis added; rev'd on other grounds, 56 F.3d 234 (D.C. Cir. 1995).[6]

Notwithstanding these express duties imposed upon the SBA in favor of small businesses, and particularly Section 8(a) concerns, the record evidence demonstrates that the SBA failed to fulfill these duties to JCA. This is shown by the SBA's utter and complete failure to respond to JCA's multiple pleas for guidance and assistance from late September 1995 through early January 1996. Indeed, the record evidence demonstrates that SBA sat idly by and did nothing at all during this lengthy period to assist its Section 8(a) contractor.

By September of 1995, JCA had begun to encounter problems with the contract. For example, JCA began to experience difficulties, both with obtaining payment from the INS and with satisfying the demands for information that were being imposed upon JCA by the INS's agent, the Defense Contract Audit Agency ("DCAA").

To seek guidance and assistance in resolving these problems, JCA's president, Joseph Cooper, immediately contacted the SBA for assistance. First, in late September 1995, Mr. Cooper telephoned SBA representatives to obtain guidance on and assistance with the payment and audit issues.[7] No SBA representatives, however, ever responded

---

6 In its opinion the Court of Appeals dismissed plaintiffs' claims from the Federal district court for lack of jurisdiction, but indicated that plaintiffs' contractual claims could have been appropriate in the Claims Court. See *A & S Council Oil Co.*, 56 F.3d at 241–42.
7 As the SBA's BOS, Ms. Collins had the critical duty of rendering assistance, arranging for additional assistance from all available sources, and coordinating the SBA's assistance to JCA under the Section 8(a). SBA SOP, "Chapter 5—Servicing the 8(a) Concern," ¶ 37 ("Business Development") at 121–22; see generally 13 C.F.R. § 124.100 (1995) (defining the BOS as the "field office employee responsible for providing business development assistance to [Section 8(a)] Program Participants").

reasonably to JCA's telephone calls with any advice or assistance.[8]

Next, after no one from the SBA had provided any guidance or assistance in response to JCA's telephone requests, on October 20, 1995, JCA sent a written request to the BOS for assistance with the problems that JCA was having under the contract. In pertinent part, JCA informed the SBA that the INS's failure to issue task orders to JCA had presented a "serious financial problem" for JCA and that JCA, "as a small business...[could not] withstand the level of delinquency that INS ha[d] imposed though failure to process invoices in a timely manner, or failure to release tasks in sufficient quantity to allow JCA to be successful." JCA's October 20, 1995, letter also specifically requested the SBA's assistance in arranging a tripartite meeting among JCA, the SBA, and the INS to address the issues that had arisen under the contract. Again, JCA received no aid, assistance, or guidance from the SBA within a reasonable time. Instead, Ms. Collins relayed JCA's requests for assistance to the SBA's 8(a) contract office.

Additionally, from October 5, 1995, through late November 1995, JCA forwarded to the SBA a courtesy copy of at least eleven letters that JCA had sent to the INS regarding the myriad of serious difficulties that JCA was having with the INS. No one from the INS responded with reasonable promptness to this correspondence. In fact, no one from the SBA responded to JCA with any offer of guidance or assistance until January 1996—well over three months after JCA began requesting the SBA's assistance.

As a party to the contract, the SBA owed to JCA, among other duties, the duty to perform in conformance with the

---

8 SBA's Section 8(a) Program...Similar to the BOS, the SBA's Contracts Office had the duty to assist In her deposition, Ms. Collins, recalled forwarding all of the correspondence to the Contracts Division of the Section 8(a) contractor. See SBA SOP, "Chapter 1 – Introduction," ¶ 4 ("General Responsibilities"), at 21–22.

SBA's enabling statute, its regulations, and its SOP with regard to the Section 8(a) program. (See, e.g., *Allenfield Assocs.*, 40 Fed. Cl. at 482; "applicable laws are binding on parties...in the context of a contract with the Federal Government, regardless of whether or not the laws are specifically incorporated into the contract.")

In the case at hand, the undisputed record demonstrates that for a period of over three months, the SBA completely failed to respond to JCA's multiple written and oral pleas for guidance and assistance with the difficulties that JCA was encountering with the INS, failed to help or assist JCA with working out problems with the DCAA, failed to make any effort to ensure that the INS understood its obligations to its Section 8(a) contractor, and otherwise failed to ensure that the INS treated JCA fairly with regard to receiving payment for work already performed or with regard to INS's handling of the DCAA's audits of JCA. By the SBA's complete and inexplicable inaction during this period, it failed to fulfill its duties to JCA, as those duties were (and are) expressly set forth in the SBA Statute and the SBA Regulations and, thereby, breached its contract with JCA. *Allenfield Assoc.*, supra.

2. The SBA Failed to Ensure that the Task Orders Issued by the INS under the Contract Were "Fair and Reasonable," and Represented a "Fair Market Price"

SBA's regulations impose upon that agency the duty to ensure that contracts awarded to Section 8(a) concerns will enable such concerns to perform the contract and "earn a reasonable profit" (13 C.F.R. § 124.307(a) (1995), "Contractual assistance"). These regulations also provide that the agency that issues the task orders to an 8(a) concern is obligated to issue them at a "fair market price" (13

C.F.R. § 124.315 (1995)). Additionally, the regulations provide that, when appropriate, SBA should request that agencies such as the INS demonstrate to the SBA—by submission of written material to the SBA—that such agencies have used appropriate methods, such as commercial prices for similar products, when determining the "fair market price" (13 C.F.R. § 124.315 (1995)). The SBA's implementing regulations state in pertinent part:

> (a) A "fair market price" for an 8(a) contract shall be determined by the agency offering the requirement to SBA in accordance with paragraphs (a)(1) and (a)(2) of this section.
>
> (b) Upon the request of SBA, an agency offering a procurement requirement for potential award through the 8(a) program shall submit to SBA a written statement detailing the method used by the agency to estimate the current fair market price for the contract (13 C.F.R. § 124.315 (1995), "Fair Market price for 8(a) awards," (emphasis added).

See also SBA SOP ¶ 99(j), pp. 263–65, Plaintiff's Appendix, Tab 70, pp. 0000469-0000471. In fact, the SBA contracting officer acknowledged that, pursuant to these provisions, the SBA would ask an agency to provide the basis for the agency's estimate of the fair market price of services in the event that the cost or price of an item became a "major issue" under the SBA contract.

On or about March 19, 1996, the INS offered JCA the opportunity to perform three new task orders, among which was a task order ("Task Order No. 2") that involved the development of black-and-white and full-color ads for the U.S. Border Patrol. This was the first task order that the INS had proposed to issue to JCA in over five months, and SBA officials knew that these proposed task orders were critical, because they represented the INS's reluctant decision to give JCA one more chance to perform.

On April 19, 1996, JCA submitted a proposal to perform Task Order No. 2 for a price of $58,024.76, which included a 10 percent profit. Upon receipt of JCA's price proposal for Task Order No. 2, however, the INS's Contracting Officer Technical Representative ("COTR"), Ms. Ellie Miller, complained that the task order should not be issued to JCA, because JCA's proposed price was "outrageous." Ms. Miller based her opinion regarding JCA's alleged outrageous price upon the fact that she had solicited a single, informal, nonbinding offer from a JCA competitor, claiming it could perform the task for $5,667.

After receiving JCA's proposal for Task Order No. 2, the INS went through the motions of conducting price negotiations with JCA. During the negotiations, JCA explained to the INS that its price position for the performance of Task Order No. 2 was so extremely low as to be "far off base." JCA explained that it could not reasonably perform Task Order No. 2 for any amount significantly less than the approximately $58,000 price that it had originally proposed. The INS, however, refused to issue Task Order No. 2 to JCA because JCA refused to reduce its proposed price to perform the task order. Subsequently, the INS obtained an independent evaluation of the cost to perform Task Order No. 2. This independent evaluation estimated that Task Order No. 2 should have cost "$75K versus the $57K quoted by [JCA.]."

The SBA was informed of the negotiations over Task Order No. 2 and knew of the INS's belief that JCA's proposed price was so excessively high as to be "outrageous." Yet, despite this knowledge, the SBA never endeavored to determine whether the INS's price negotiations were based on a "fair market price."

In fact, the SBA never attempted to request any information whatsoever from the INS to determine how the INS arrived at its estimate for a fair market price for Task Order No. 2.

By this complete lack of action to determine whether the price that the INS attempted to impose upon JCA was a reasonable "fair market price," the SBA once again failed to fulfill its duties to JCA, as those duties were expressly set forth in the SBA Statute and the SBA Regulations, thereby again breaching its contract with JCA. (*Allenfield Assocs.*, 40 Fed. Cl. 471.)

B. The SBA Breached Its Implied Contractual Duties to JCA by the SBA's Unreasonable Failure to Cooperate with JCA to Respond to JCA's Repeated Requests for Assistance

Apart from, and in addition to, the SBA's statutory and regulatory duties to JCA, the SBA also owed JCA the duty under common law to provide "reasonable cooperation" with JCA in its efforts to perform the contract. The SBA failed to fulfill this duty as well.

Parties to a government contract are bound by the implied duty of good faith and fair dealing (*Celeron Gathering Corp*, 34 Fed. Cl. at 752; see also Restatement (Second) of Contracts § 205 (1981), every contract imposes upon each party an obligation of good faith). The concept of fair dealing imposes upon the government:

> a duty to render reasonable cooperation to the contractor in the performance of the contract and an additional duty not to hinder the contractor's performance. *A claim under the duty of cooperation concerns the reasonableness of the government's actions* after considering the facts and circumstances

at the time. *(Celeron Gathering Corp.,* 34 Fed. Cl. at 753 (finding that government acted unreasonably); emphasis added, citation omitted; see also *George A. Fuller Co. v. United States,* 108 Ct. Cl. 70, 94, 69 F. Supp. 409, 411 (1947)).

Moreover, good faith performance or enforcement of a contract emphasizes "faithfulness to an agreed common purpose and consistency with the justified expectations of the other party" (Restatement (Second) Contracts § 205, cmt. (a) (1981)).

Pursuant to the standard articulated under Celeron and the Restatement, JCA, as an 8(a) contractor in a tripartite contract with the SBA and INS, had the reasonable and justified expectation that the SBA would fulfill its purpose in the 8(a) program by cooperating with and assisting JCA when difficulties arose with INS. Yet, as was exhaustively detailed in the Argument portion of this brief at Argument Section II.A.1, supra, the SBA failed on numerous occasions to cooperate with and otherwise assist JCA so as not to hinder JCA's performance of the contract. There was nothing reasonable about the SBA's inexplicable action of refusing to acknowledge JCA's pleas for assistance and guidance for over 3 months. Moreover, as discussed herein at Argument Section II.A.2, there was nothing reasonable about the SBA's decision to sit on its hands and do nothing to ensure that the INS was offering to pay JCA a fair market price for its services, particularly in this instance, where JCA was being given only one final chance to perform.

Through these series of critical failings, the SBA cannot be said to have acted reasonably under the circumstances. The SBA completely failed to fulfill contractual duties to JCA and, thus, breached its contract with JCA.

U.S. COURT OF FEDERAL CLAIMS
No. 00-323C
FILED: July 12, 2002
J. COOPER & ASSOCIATES, INC.,
Plaintiff v.
UNITED STATES, Defendant
Indefinite Delivery, Indefinite Quantity Contract; Letter Contract Cross-Motion for Summary Judgment; Presumption of Good Faith Performance by Government Officials

I believe that my problems in obtaining justice in the court system started with the decision of Judge Marian Blank Horn, of the U.S. Court of Federal Claims. I think it is safe to say that I have not suffered injustice without learning for sure what justice truly is. I cannot explain why Judge Horn decided not to rule in my favor. I am sure she would say that it was a question of law. However, the facts and evidence in the case leave any reasonable person to wonder how and why she arrived at some of her conclusions. I have read Judge Horn's decision many times and still fail to understand how she interpreted the law. I am not a lawyer, but I consider myself a reasonably intelligent person. I can tell the difference between what is right and what is wrong.

Judges are not supreme. They do make mistakes. There were numerous existing legislative and executive remedies already on the books, so the only decision Judge Horn had to execute was to ask why SBA did not implement the Business Opportunity Development Reform Act of 1988 (P.L. 100-656) or implement the FAR regulations, particularly because the Department of Justice IG issued an investigative report, dated August 1977, which confirmed that contractors misrepresented their small business status in order to acquire contract set-aside for JCA.

JCA clearly demonstrated to the U.S. Court of Federal Claims that, under the common law of contracts, the government had breached its contractual duty of good faith and fair dealing, where the INS program and contracting officials either knew or had reason to know that JCA 's competitors had falsely certified themselves as small, disadvantaged businesses—yet the INS officials continued to contract with those competitors to JCA's detriment.

The crucial issue placed before the court was whether the INS's conduct in this case constituted a breach of contract under federal contract law. The court, in turn, relied upon the questionable, but often cited, proposition that, in order to demonstrate that the government failed to act in good faith, the contractor must prove that the government acted in *"bad faith."* Under the *"bad faith"* standard, the contractor must show *"irrefragable proof"* that the government official acted with specific disposition against the contractor—a virtually impossible standard to meet.

Subsequent to the JCA case, the court has definitively ruled that a contractor is no longer required to demonstrate that the government acted in *"bad faith"* in order to prevail on a breach-of-contract claim predicated upon the government's failure to act in good faith. Unfortunately, for JCA, this long-overdue ruling arrived much too late.

In the section "The Argument as Presented to the Court," I have gone into great detail about my argument before Judge Horn, regarding why and how the SBA and INS, working in collusion with large contractors, destroyed my former business. I would like to touch on a few of the court decisions because of the importance Judge Horn placed on them in arriving at her conclusions.

IDIQ CONTRACT:

Both the INS and JCA stated before the court that JCA contract was contemplated to become an IDIQ contract and that JCA's contract had to be definitized before that could occur, which was never done. The government argued. However, because the letter contract had a minimum guaranteed with JCA of $250,000, and the government met that minimum guarantee, that was enough to make JCA's contract an IDIQ contract, even though the contract did not have the FAR 52.216-22 requirements and was not definitized, which was required. The government argued that regardless of what else happened in the administration of the contract, INS met all the obligations that it had to JCA, pursuant to the IDIQ contract. Therefore, JCA's contract had been satisfied.

When the INS argues before the court that it owes JCA nothing because they met the minimum guarantee, one has to ask oneself: does meeting the minimum guarantee give the INS the right to break the law? Does it give the INS the right to participate in the destruction of a small, minority-owned business? Does it give the SBA and INS the right to ignore laws passed by Congress? The INS and SBA should not be in the business of destroying small businesses to protect special interests, which I believe is what happened in JCA's case.

When JCA entered into the tripartite agreement with the SBA and INS, it was never JCA's understanding that if problems were to arise between the parties, all FAR regulations and SBA policies impacting the SBA 8(a) program would be void or ignored. It was never JCA's understanding that the

Business Opportunity Development Reform Act of 1988 (P.L. 100-656) would be ignored or violated.

JCA's principal argument before the court was that JCA's INS contract was a requirements contract—or, simply put, a letter contract with a minimum guarantee. Because INS requirement was of an urgent nature in order to get started immediately, a letter contract accompanied the INS solicitation letter to the SBA. The FAR states "[a] letter contract is a written preliminary contractual instrument that authorizes the contractor to begin immediately manufacturing supplies or performing services." 48C.F.R. 16.603-1 (1995). The letter contract states that an IDIQ contract was contemplated and indicated that the contract would be definitized in the future by the parties, but not later than October 16, 1995. I believe my argument before the Claims Court was correct in that JCA contract was not an IDIQ contract as stipulated by FAR regulations, in her court testimony, Michelle Wall, INS contracting officer, stated:

Wall Deposition-Responding to JCA attorney's questions.

Q: So what kind of contract was the letter contract?

A: The letter contract strictly allows the contractor to start work immediately.

Q: Was a letter contract an IDIQ contract?

MR. SIMKIN: Objection, calls for a legal conclusion.

Q: I need your understanding as a contracting officer, Ms. Wall.

A: Was the letter contract an IDIQ contract.

Q: Yes

A: Let me think about this for a second, because
            the letter contract in and of itself may be rep-
            resentative of one thing versus the actual final
            contract. Because the letter contract, in and
            of itself, has its own terms and conditions and
            then the final defines. The contract has its own
            terms and conditions. I'm going to say no.

Judge Horn ruled that the letter contract between the parties was an IDIQ contract, which guaranteed only $250,000
of work to JCA. She did not consider any of the FAR regulations or the Business Opportunity Development Reform Act
of 1988 (P.L. 100-656), which was also violated by the government, when making her decision. It is clear she did not
consider any of the SBA policies affecting SBA 8(a) contractors important.

DISSATISFIED WITH JCA PERFORMANCE:

JCA's contract required definitization, unless the government exercised its contract termination authority. The
clauses provided that in the event the parties could not
agree on a proper rate, the agency would unilaterally set
the rate. The INS breached the contract when it failed to
definitize the contract promised in the letter contract and
required by law.

As an excuse, INS argued before the court that JCA's
contract was never definitized, because the INS was not
satisfied with JCA's performance and had questions about
JCA's pricing, which led to the INS hiring DCAA to conduct

audits on JCA's invoices and accounting system. Judge Horn addressed these two arguments heavily in reaching her decision. However, on the question of the INS being **dissatisfied with JCA's performance,** there's plenty of evidence to the contrary, which Judge Horn did not take into consideration when making her decision.

Joseph Garforth, senior INS contracting officer, testified that JCA did nothing wrong regarding performance, and when he asked the INS program staff to give him evidence of JCA's poor work performance, the program staff could not provide any data. In addition, the INS never put in writing (either to the SBA or JCA) its dissatisfaction with JCA's performance, which is required by FAR regulations. In fact, the INS approved and accepted all work presented by JCA without any complaints.

Garforth Deposition: Responding to JCA attorney's questions.

Q: I'm curious. Do you recall any reason why INS would have been reluctant at this time to inform JCA about performance problems?

A: If there were problems, they should have been—I don't know—I—all I can tell you is I heard the program office complained at times, and all they wanted to do was see the backup.

Q: You wanted to see the backup?

A: Right.

Q. You being the contracting official? You wanted to see the backup?

A: Right.

Q: Do you have any idea why the program officials were not providing the backup?

A: No, I don't.

Q: So until the program officials could provide backup you really couldn't say anything? You couldn't provide any guidance to Cooper, is that correct?

A: Correct. I mean what are they doing wrong?

In the DOJ IG Investigative Report dated July 23, 1997, regarding the interview of Andrea K. Grimsley, INS contracting officer, Ms. Grimsley states: "...the Program Office was not happy with JCA's work, which they felt was not professional. However, the Program Office never put JCA on notice of their disapproval with this work performance. Instead, the Program Office maintained signing off and approving these work invoices." Carol Hall, INS program director, sent an e-mail dated September 19, 1995, to her staff advising that more money would be needed for JCA's contract, because JCA was doing a lot of work. Nowhere in her e-mail does she mention that JCA's work performance was unsatisfactory.

The INS could not support its charges of JCA's work as being "unprofessional." The court should have admonished the INS for not following FAR regulations by putting in writing its complaints with JCA's work performance. Logically, if JCA's work was "unprofessional," why would the government approve the work and pay for the service? These complaints were just another means the INS used to justify terminating its contract with JCA.

In my opinion, the court should have investigated why the INS failed to issue written task orders, as required by the letter contract. It is significant because the INS claimed that the quality of JCA's work was poor. The INS has no basis to complain about the quality of JCA's work, when it issued vague wording and hurried task orders without the uniform written guidance required under the contract. Two INS Contracting Officers, Ms. Wall and Ms. Allen, both stated in their depositions that *"prior to hiring the new COTR, the government had no concerns over JCA performance problems."* How Judge Horn missed these very important issues is puzzling.

Unfortunately for JCA, Judge Horn agreed with the government's position, ignoring Mr. Garforth's testimony and Ms. Grimsley's admission that INS never put into writing any complaints about JCA's work performance, which was required by law. That the court would give weight to INS's complaints without supportive documentation is troubling.

JCA'S PRICING:

With respect to Judge Horn's comments about JCA's pricing, there is not much JCA can say about the matter. The letter contract specified firm, fixed-price, labor hour rates. INS was aware and approved the interim labor rates when JCA presented the numbers to INS contracting and program staff in the July 1995 meeting and discussions. At the time, the INS did not voice any objections or express any concerns. It is clear the INS approved the rates but did not understand what they had agreed to. Upon receiving JCA's invoices, the INS was shock and refused to pay them.

It is virtually unprecedented for an agency to require an audit of each invoice before the invoice is paid, as the

INS did here. The audit was wholly unjustified and served only to delay payment. The INS's actions caused great harm to JCA's financial system. The INS audited JCA's accounting system for almost a year without adequate explanation for the extended audit, which continued despite the DCAA's initial finding that JCA's accounting system was satisfactory. To this day, JCA has never been provided an explanation of why its accounting system was not adequate, other than that its invoices were not properly formatted. Linda Greene's letter dated January 22, 1996, states: "Based on your concern...regarding what constitutes an acceptable invoice for payment, we determined that your November 13, 1995, invoice with the supporting data attached is an acceptable format for invoicing." JCA used this format in future invoicing, but it was never acceptable to the INS. For some reason, Judge Horn did not see this action as bad faith on the part of the INS.

One Last Chance:

In her ruling, Judge Horn states, *"INS stated that at this point their preference is to meet their $250,000 threshold of obligation under the letter contract and terminate their involvement with this company [JCA]. However, Linda [INS Director of Contracts] stated that in all fairness to the company, she will issue them one more task to give them another chance to perform. She said that she had to urge her customer [the INS] to issue another task order in light of all the previous problems. When one of JCA resulting proposals was more than ten times an estimate the INS had obtained from one of JCA's competitors, the INS informed JCA that their proposal was unacceptable and declined to grant to JCA the task order."*

The issue of the INS giving JCA "one last chance" to perform and the INS's position that JCA price proposal for the task was arbitrarily and capriciously thought to be "outrageous", was unsupportable. In fact, there was no reasonable basis for this judgment, and JCA's price proposal was *significantly less* than a subsequent independent government estimate. In formulating its estimate, "the government must act in good faith and use reasonable care in computing its estimated needs; it is not free to carelessly guess at its needs."

Actually, the INS breached the letter contract when "Linda" stated in the meeting on February 12, 1996, that the INS would "give the company one more chance to perform." Linda stated that the "company will have to produce superior work at this point to turn their current image around." DCAA employees in attendance at the meeting noted that an advertisement deserving of a "Cleo Award" in the commercial world was the term used by INS to describe the superiority of the work the company must submit at this time for the INS to even consider any other work with JCA. Thus, as the INS imposed a requirement for performance that was in excess of what was called for by the contract, it breached that contract. I was surprised that Judge Horn did not pick this fact up. She should have. One just can't change a contract verbally without some form of written amendment to that contract.

DCAA-JCA ACCOUNTING SYSTEM:

The DCAA documents provided to JCA in response to its FOIA request reflect the agency's predisposition against JCA. The documents show that the INS was seeking to use the audit process to avoid its obligation to definitize the contract and to deny JCA the costs it incurred at the direction of the INS. After its acceptance of these initial deliverables, INS misled JCA into believing that it intended to definitize the contract, and that it intended to issue future work orders to JCA. For example, in October or November 1995, JCA was directed to replace its accounting system with a system that would make it easier for the DCAA to audit invoices in the future. During the time that the INS and DCAA were telling JCA to replace its accounting system, the INS was actually diverting work from JCA's contract to other companies not under the 8(a) program. Not only was the INS breaking the law, it was also acting in bad faith.

The lack of good faith is further documented in internal INS memoranda. On August 27, 1996, following completion of the contract's base year, the contracting officer, John Russo, urged the INS to develop a negotiation position. Mr. Russo states: "[w]e can't leave Mr. Cooper hanging because he is going to know from the out-brief DCAA [will] provide that the audit stage is over, and we're up next." In a brief postscript, Mr. Russo reveals his intentions to avoid definitization when he comments on the results of the subsequent audit: "I read the audit report. It is exactly what I had hoped for." "This audit report criticized JCA's accounting system, contradicting a prior audit that found the accounting system acceptable." This clearly shows bad faith on the part of Russo toward JCA. He demonstrates bias and lack of objectivity. Reading Russo's May 16, 1996, letter to the SBA and reading his deposition, it is clear he was not a friend of JCA. He lied about issuing contracts to non-8(a) contractors, and his actions violated the FAR 13.204(a) (1995) and the Business Opportunity Development Reform Act of 1988 (P.L. 100-656).

The INS's objective was clearly to create a cloud of doubt concerning JCA's qualifications to perform the INS contract.

It was very difficult for JCA to overcome the many lies and misleading statements the INS put out to the public—diverting attention from the laws it had violated working in collusions with major companies (J. Walter Thompson, Bernard Hodes, and CASS Communications) that represented themselves as disadvantaged businesses in order to acquire the contract set aside for JCA.

The INS suggested that it had good reason to refuse to definitize the letter contract, because the DCAA had determined that the "JCA accounting system was inadequate in some respects for accumulating, segregating, and reporting costs under government contracts." The INS studiously ignored the irrefutable record fact that, notwithstanding the DCAA's informal comments on JCA's accounting system, on December 7, 1995, the DCAA had issued a formal audit report, in which the DCAA expressly determined that JCA's accounting system was "acceptable for the award of the prospective contract" with a "recommendation that a follow-on accounting system review be performed after contract award."

The INS's unfounded allegations about the inadequacies of JCA's accounting system also ignored the DCAA's September 16, 1996, audit report, in which it expressly acknowledged as follows: "JCA utilizes a computerized job cost accounting system. The accounting system has controls to effectively identify and segregate unallowable costs. We consider the contractor's accounting system adequate because the system is designed to accumulate and segregate direct costs by contract and indirect costs by cost pool."

The INS used the DCAA to create a justification for allowing JCA's contract to lapse. In a meeting on February

12, 1996, "INS asked DCAA what will happen once the company (JCA) claims to have the requested documentation. We explained to her that we will review everything in their books at one time, at one place. Whatever the company is able to submit at that time will be taken into consideration and whatever is not will be considered unsupported or unresolved. We will issue an opinion, most likely adverse, advising INS not to negotiate." This discussion between DCAA and INS does not sound like the INS was acting in good faith toward JCA. In the end, the second approval from DCAA Audit Report No. 6221-96B11070100, Section 1 Recommendation, confirmed that JCA's accounting system was acceptable for the award of the prospective contract. The same DCAA auditors who gave JCA all the difficulties in conducting the audit are the same individuals who signed off on the recommendation.

INS WAS NOT OBLIGATED TO NOTIFY JCA/INS WAS USING NON-8 (a) FIRMS:

In her ruling, Judge Horn stated, *"The plaintiff's remaining claims that the government acted in bad faith by failing to notify JCA that it was using other contractors to fulfill needs described in the statement of work also are groundless. The government was under no obligation to inform JCA that other contractors were being used to satisfy INS needs. JCA was entitled only to the $250,000.00 minimum guarantee listed in the letter contract, regardless of the work tasked to other contractors."* The INS and the Court thus suggest that the INS lived up to its bargain by paying JCA in excess of $280,000. What Judge Horn failed to take into consideration is that the payments to JCA were late—late to the point that JCA was run out of business.

By November 13, 1995, JCA had billed the INS $331,300 for services performed under the letter contract. Through March 19, 1996, the INS paid JCA a total of $230,991 under the letter contract, less than the minimum guarantee of $250,000 for the promised definitive IDIQ contract. It was not until November 18, 1996, almost four months after the letter contract had lapsed, that JCA received $49,936, a payment with which the INS finally satisfied the $250,000 minimum guarantee of the promised definitive IDIQ contract. The fact that JCA had not acquired its full minimum guarantee of $250,000 before the contract lapse was for some reason not a concern of the court.

According to FAR regulations and SBA policies related to SDB 8(a) contractors John Russo, senior contracting officer for INS makes it clear in his letter to the SBA dated May 16, 1996, that SBA policies and regulations required the INS to notify the SBA of any modifications to the JCA contract. He is also very specific in his deposition. The INS had an obligation to notify the SBA when they decided to satisfy its requirement through non-Section 8(a) contractors.

Russo's Deposition-JCA attorney is asking the questions.

Q: Would you read that paragraph and tell me what you meant by it and what it was meant to do.

A: In my view it was intended to put the SBA on notice that our plan was to try to satisfy our requirements in some other way other than to rely on the Cooper contract, since we couldn't go anywhere with it.

Q: Why did you feel you had to provide That notice to SBA

A: Our contract was with SBA.

The INS had an obligation to advise JCA, because JCA was part of the tripartite letter contract and the subcontractor to the SBA, who was the prime contractor to the INS. Russo was fully aware of the FAR regulations. Further, in a letter to Ms. Collins, SBA BOS, from Michelle Wall, INS contracting officer, dated July 7, 1995, the INS requests permission to negotiate an IDIQ contract directly with JCA. The SBA agreed to this request. Any modification that would have potentially affected the negotiations for the IDIQ contract, JCA should have been advised of.

Another senior contracting officer for the INS, Andrea Grimsley, was aware that the INS needed the SBA's permission to use non-8(a) contractors for their requirement, as she states in the DOJ IG *Investigative Report* on July 23, 1997: "INS had sent a letter to SBA dated May 16, 1996, informing SBA that it was INS intention to terminate its contract with JCA an 8(a) set-aside contractor." She stated that she was advised by the SBA that it accepted the INS's request and that a "written letter will be following their conversation." When pressed to produce the SBA letter, Grimsley stated she could not find a copy. She called the SBA and was informed that they could not find a letter giving the INS the authority to use non-8(a) contractors to meet the INS requirement. When the INS informed the court that it had SBA *"concurrence"* to use non-8(a) contractors to implement its requirement, it was a lie. The court failed to require the INS to support its claim. The court decided that JCA was not telling the truth and ruled in favor of INS. Once again Judge Horn was misled in part because of her naive belief that government officials "Carry out their duties lawfully and in good faith." Instead of asking INS to support its position with documents, she blindly accepted whatever the INS told her.

I must question all of Judge Horn's decisions, particularly when she writes, *"the court proceed from a strong presumption that government officials...Carry out their duties lawfully and in good faith."* She makes clear her feelings about the government acting in bad faith when, in oral arguments before her on March 5, 2002, JCA states: "It was bad faith for the INS to obtain public relations and advertising support service...." Judge Horn states: "Well, we are not going to talk about bad faith here...we do not have enough in the record right now to show bad faith...but you are not going to get real far with a bad faith argument...."

I was troubled by these particular comments from Judge Horn, because if there is one thing JCA has done in this case, it is to show just how much the INS not only lied and broke the law but also injured JCA by working in bad faith. And it was intentional. The INS violated the Business Opportunity Development Reform Act of 1988 (P.L. 100-656), when it participated in giving contracts set aside for JCA to large companies—giving contracts to large companies claiming to be small, disadvantaged businesses. The INS helped these contractors sign government orders, making this claim. This was a violation of the law.

It was collusion. It was a lie, it was fraud, and the law was broken. I recognize that the U.S. Court of Federal Claims does not have jurisdiction over fraud issues. Nevertheless, the INS was working in bad faith against JCA. The court stated, "There is no evidence of specific intent to injure" JCA. There is no indication in the record of bad faith on the part of INS officials. Having said all the above, I must wonder how Judge Horn could state that "...government officials...Carry out their duties lawfully and in good faith." Judges sometimes think about the institution in terms of protecting it, while failing to think about the individuals who are harmed and need protection. With her decision, Judge Horn would appear to be more concerned with protecting special-interest groups or the institution.

Judge Marian Horn's ruling was that JCA's INS contract was an IDIQ contract with a $250,000 minimum guaranteed, which the INS met; and as a result of INS meeting this guarantee, the INS had no further responsibility to JCA. Judge Horn ignored some basic facts and evidence in arriving at her decision. She completely ignored all the relevant FAR 52.216-22 regulations that are required to make a letter contract into an IDIQ contract. She completely ignored the fact that JCA's letter contract was set aside and accepted by the SBA for JCA, a SBA 8(a) contractor. No modifications could take place with JCA's INS contract without the SBA's written approval, particularly as the contract was a tripartite contract between the INS, SBA, and JCA. Finally, Judge Horn refused to acknowledge that JCA's contract could not be an IDIQ contract, as the contract had not been definitized.

I cannot explain why or how the U.S. Court of Appeals for the Federal Circuit affirms her decision. I can only say it was very frustrating to see how the law was ignored by those responsible to enforce it. I was disappointed—justice failed me.

U.S. DISTRICT COURT FOR THE DISTRICT OF COLUMBIA UNITED STATES OF AMERICA, ex rel. J. COOPER & ASSOCIATES, INC.
    PLAINTIFF,
    V.
BERNARD HODES GROUP, INC.,
CASS COMMUNICATIONS, INC., AND J. WALTER THOMPSON CO.
    DEFENDANTS

CIVIL ACTION No.: 03-2436 (RMU)

On March 23, 2006, the U.S. District Court for the District of Columbia handed down a decision regarding my complaint, which was not favorable. I believe strongly to this day that what happened to my former business was a great injustice. I believe the government's actions and the defendants' behavior were shameful and harmful to every small, disadvantaged business in this country.

District Judge Ricardo M. Urbina acknowledged in his decision that the defendants, J. Walter Thompson, Bernard Hodes Group, and CASS Communications, did misrepresent themselves as "disadvantaged" businesses, when, in fact, they were not. He further ruled that *"The evidence in this case shows that the INS was aware that the defendants were not small and or disadvantaged businesses and offered them advertising and public relations contracts anyway."* When I read the decision, I thought the Judge had swallowed his sandwich without chewing it. I could not believe it. The ruling essentially said that I was right; the companies were not small—but so what?

I was surprised to learn that if the government participates or is aware of a crime being committed, then it is not a crime, and the government cannot be held accountable. That is what happened in my case. The court ruled, *"The government's decision to award contracts to the defendants, despite its knowledge that the defendants were not small or disadvantaged businesses, negates any claim of fraud against the defendants."* A couple of things stand out in Judge Urbina's decision that are worth mentioning. First, the court acknowledged that large corporations did indeed misrepresent their small business status. Second, the court stated that numerous media reports on the defendants would suffice to *"set government investigators on the trail of fraud,"* and third, the court stated, *"During the course of the plaintiff's suit against the government however, the INS explicitly admitted that it "obtained with the concurrence of SBA, some advertising services from other vendors outside the section 8(a) program" and even named defendant JWT as one such vendor."*

Like Judge Horn, Judge Urbina never questioned the government to determine if what they argued was true. The INS never obtained SBA's "concurrence" to use non-Section 8(a) contractors to implement the INS requirement. On May 16, 1996, the INS letter to the SBA was the first time the INS notified the SBA that it planned to use non-Section 8(a) contractors for the INS requirement. The INS had been using non-Section 8(a) contractors who were claiming to be disadvantaged businesses for months prior to the May 16, 1996, letter. As I stated earlier, in the U.S. Court of Federal Claims' decision, the INS could never produce any written documents from the SBA authorizing the INS to use non-Section 8(a) contractors to implement its requirement. Verbal authorization is not sufficient for such a modification of a SBA 8(a) set-aside contract. FAR regulations and SBA policies require written authorization from the SBA to the INS to implement such modifications. This never occurred.

Even though the court ruled that the contractors did not commit fraud under the False Claims Act, the Business

Opportunity Development Reform Act of 1988 (P.L. 100-656) had been violated, along with numerous FAR Regulations. The court made no mention of these violations. The court did suggest that the government investigators should explore fraud. However, given this decision, neither the SBA IG nor DOJ IG took any action to resolve this issue.

ORIGINAL SOURCE:

One of the major questions before the court was whether the "Original Source" was JCA or the DOJ IG Investigative Report. The court used a formula in arriving at its decision. The formula X (misrepresented state of facts) +Y (true state of facts) = Z (fraud): *You need either X or Y to proceed. Y is clearly in the public domain because knowledge of the size of the ad agencies is publicly available. And X is in the public domain because JCA is (the original source) who put it there, and doing so resulted in the DOJ IG Investigative Report. JCA get to claim X if JCA is the original source (no question about that), but once DOJ declines to take the case over, JCA proceed only if JCA have "contributed significant independent information," or if JCA have "elements of new wrongful transactions or [can introduce] material elements to the publicly disclosed transaction."* The court stated that "...there is no requirement...that the relevant public disclosures irrefutably prove a case of fraud. It is sufficient that the 'publicly disclosed transaction is sufficient to raise the inference of fraud.'"

In 1996, JCA raised the issue of fraud with the DOJ IG, along with JCA's attorney, Jed Babbin, of Tighe, Patton, Tabackman & Babbin, LLP. Jed Babbin and I met with Dave Glendening, DOJ IG, at 1:00 p.m., February 1, 1996, at Glendening's office, 1425 New York Avenue, NW, Washington, DC. Babbin and I discussed the fact that several white-owned firms were misrepresenting themselves as small, minority-owned businesses; in fact, I gave two names to Glendening—J. Walter Thompson and Bernard Hodes, two of the contractors in question. Glendening was told that these firms were multimillion-dollar companies. In addition, I provided Glendening with copies of blanket purchasing agreements, signed contracts by the contractors claiming to be small "disadvantaged" minority businesses. In addition, we provided Glendening with the FAR regulations that had been violated, along with the Business Opportunity Reform Development Act of 1988 (P.L. 100-656). With this information, the DOJ IG started its investigation into JCA's complaint. During the investigation, the DOJ IG never spoke to me or any of the JCA staff.

With the information I've outlined above, I find it hard to understand how the court could take the position that JCA was not the original source, considering JCA was the one to provide the DOJ IG with the information to start its investigation.

Court Statements

Perhaps the decision of the court that I find most difficult to accept is the following statement by the judge: *"The Plaintiff is Not an Original Source of Any Information Underlying the Allegation."* The court further states, *"Although the plaintiff did write to the OIG in January 1997 that 'several large white firms misrepresented themselves...in order to obtain contracts with the [INS],' this vague statement fails to demonstrate that the plaintiff had any knowledge of alleged wrongdoing by the particular defendants.*[9] *United States*

_____

[9] "It is also possible that the plaintiff's letters to the OIG and the SBA provided the impetus for the OIG investigation. Defs.' Mot. At 18. This fact alone, however, does not assist the plaintiff in meeting the burden of establishing the court's subject-matter jurisdiction. Although the plaintiff may have communicated vague suspicions of fraudulent practices by unnamed entities, it was the OIG that uncovered, through its own investigations, the identities of the alleged perpetrators and the exact circumstances of their allegedly fraudulent acts."

ex rel. Kinney v. Stoltz, 327 F.3d 671, 675 (8th Cir.2003) (stating that knowledge of fraudulent practices in general is not sufficient to overcome the FCA's jurisdictional bar, and that a plaintiff must demonstrate direct and independent knowledge of the role played by the particular defendants). Finally, Judge Urbina stated that *"the defendants' statements to the INS employee confirming their small or disadvantaged business status and the designation of the defendants as 'Disadvantaged' on the government-issued orders is admittedly 'curious.'"*

For some reason I thought the information (evidence) I and my lawyer supplied to the DOJ IG was sufficient to prove that JCA was the "original source" to the government, regarding the defendants' misrepresenting their small business status. JCA supplied the names of the violators, J. Walter Thompson and Bernard Hodes Group; JCA supplied copies of the contracts (BPA); and JCA supplied information on the size of these contractors and much more to the government. The court stated: *"In addition, the plaintiff does not argue that it is the original source of the information regarding the size and wealth of the defendant businesses that was disclosed in various media reports, ('X + Y' = Z). Further, there is no evidence in the record that the plaintiff provided—or could have provided—any media outlets with this information."*

There is no question that the District Court decision went completely over my head. To this day, I am still wondering how the "formula" affects, explains away, or justifies how government contractors can get away with fraud, misrepresenting themselves as "disadvantaged" businesses to illegally acquire contracts set-aside for small businesses in the SBA 8(a) program. I am having a great deal of trouble understanding how a crime can be committed, and yet it isn't a crime if the government is aware of the crime. How or why the court never addressed or mentioned the violation of the Business Opportunity Development Reform Act of 1988 (P.L. 100-656) is puzzling to me.

Despite what the District Court ruled regarding *"vague statements of wrongdoing, fail to demonstrate that the plaintiff had any knowledge of alleged wrongdoing,"* and that JCA was not the "original source," JCA was in fact the first to bring to the government's attention that a violation of law (fraud) had taken place against the federal government, affecting the JCA/INS/SBA 8(a) set-aside contract. The evidence JCA submitted to the Court was based on "direct and independent knowledge" of the role the contractors played in this matter. I have read Judge Urbina's decision several times, and I have no idea what the judge took into consideration in making his decision. It makes no sense to me. I have spoken to many lawyers, and I have yet to find one who can explain Judge Urbina's decision with a straight face.

FEDERAL ACQUISITION REGULATIONS (FAR):

It has been well documented that the FAR has the force of law. Applicable provisions of the FAR are incorporated into every federal government procurement contract and have the same effect as if they were set forth in the contract itself. The FAR is very specific on how federal 8(a) minority contractors are to perform and equally specific on how the government should perform when it comes to administering an 8(a) set-aside contract (FAR 19.501 (G)).

Both the INS and SBA contracting officers ignored the FAR with respect to monitoring and implementing the JCA-INS contract. Specifically, these agencies ignored the FAR regulations and their impact on the JCA contract in the following ways:

A. INS issuance of Blanket Purchasing Agreements (BPA) and Small Purchases under the 8(a) program to circumvent the procurement system. B. INS modification of an existing 8(a) set-aside contract without the SBA's written approval. C. SBA failure to provide guidance, technical assistance, and managerial assistance to an 8(a) contractor.

BPA-INS VIOLATION:

The INS violated the FAR provisions governing simplified acquisition procedures by awarding contracts to firms other than JCA through BPA. The FAR provides that simplified acquisition procedures, which include the use of BPAs, cannot be used if the government's acquisition of supplies or services is initially expected to exceed the simplified acquisition threshold. (See FAR 13.101 (1995)).

It is undisputed that the value of the INS requirement under which JCA performed was estimated to total $8 million. The undisputed facts confirm that, despite the fact that the estimated value of the INS requirement unquestionably exceeded the applicable simplified acquisition procedure threshold, the INS nevertheless proceeded to use BPAs to order tens and perhaps hundreds of thousands of dollars' worth of services to satisfy the requirement.

In order to get around the procurement process and award contracts to certain firms, the INS contracting officer misrepresented that nonminority firms were in fact minority

firms. Some of the firms in question were Abramson, Ehrlich & Manes, CASS Recruitment Publication, Bernard Hodes, and J. Walter Thompson. Specialized Communications. None of these firms are minority-owned or disadvantaged businesses, yet the INS represented to the world that they were. There is no question that the INS violated the regulations governing the FAR's simplified acquisition procedure.

BUSINESS OPPORTUNITY DEVELOPMENT REFORM ACT OF 1988 (Public law 100-656):

In addition to violating the FAR regulations, INS violated the Business Opportunity Reform Act of 1988 (Public law 100-656).

124.1011   What is a *misrepresentation* of SBA Status

a)   Any person or entity that *misrepresents* a firm's status as a "small business concern owned and controlled by Socially and economically disadvantaged individuals" ("SDB status") in order to obtain an 8(a) or SDB contracting opportunity or preference will be subject to the penalties imposed by section 16 (d) of the Small Business Act, 15 U.S.C. 645 (d), as well as any other penalty authorized law.

b)   A representation of SDB status by any firm that SBA has found not to be an SDB (either in connection with an SDB application or protest) will be deemed a misrepresentation of SDB status, unless and until the firm reapplies for and obtains SDB certification.

PENALTIES

The Act provides for felony convictions, imprisonment up to ten years and/or criminal fines of up to $500,000, mandatory three years' debarment, and forfeitures for companies that are found to have misrepresented their small business status.

INS VIOLATED SET-ASIDE REQUIREMENT USE OF BPA:

The INS violated the FAR provisions mandating that the INS provide notice to the SBA, once the INS had determined to satisfy its requirement with non-Section 8(a) concerns. The FAR mandates that an agency must provide **written notice to the SBA** if it decides to withdraw or modify its small business set-asides determination (FAR 19.506(c), 1995). As demonstrated below, the INS violated this requirement by failing to notify the SBA of its decision to order services for its requirement from non-Section 8(a) concerns.

The INS determination and finding for authorization to contract for the requirement proved that it intended to procure the entire requirement from the SBA Section 8(a) program. The INS offered the entire requirement to the SBA Section 8(a) program, and the SBA accepted the entire requirement as a set-aside procurement for the Section 8(a) program. A memorandum dated April 23, 1996, mentions a meeting where the SBA's Shapleigh Drisco informs the INS that "once a requirement is offered to an 8(a) program, it remains an 8(a) requirement unless INS could provide a strong justification for withdrawal." Nothing in the letter contract suggested that the INS intended to award any work relating to the requirement to any contractor other than

JCA. In fact, here is the sworn testimony of Pat Collins, SBA BOS:

Collins Deposition-JCA attorney is asking the questions.

Q: Turning to your acceptance letter, did the SBA understand that it was accepting the entire requirement for JCA?

A: Yes accepting it for the 8(a) program first and then on behalf of J. Cooper and Associates for the entire period of time, because it says inclusive of all options.

Q: Now, you mentioned the term set-aside. What do you mean by that?

A: Set-aside is a—it's a sole source contract under the 8(a) program. It means it didn't have to compete for it, it was a sole source. It's a special program under the 8(a) program called set-aside. You know, we have small business set-asides, we have 8(a) set-asides, we have SBD set-asides.

Q: Did you understand this to be an 8(a) set-aside?

A: I understood it to be an 8(a) set-aside.

The INS knew, while it was diverting work from JCA to non-8(a) firms, that it was acting outside the law. Ellie Miller, INS Contracting Officer Technical Representative (COTR), states in her sworn testimony:

Miller's Deposition-JCA attorney is asking the questions.

Q: Lisa Scott. Do you remember working with Lisa Scott?

A: Yes.

Q.   Do you know how Ms. Scott got the information that J. Walter Thompson was a Disadvantaged company

A: No, I don't.

Q: Is it your understanding that J. Walter Thompson is a disadvantaged company?

A: No, he's not.

Q: Is it your understanding that Cass Recruitment is a disadvantaged company?

A: It's not my understanding that they are. I don't know one way or the other.

Q: You're fairly sure about J. Walter Thompson?

A: I'm not fairly sure; it's not my understanding they are.

As of March 13, 1996, the INS had begun ordering advertising services for its requirement through the award of task orders under a BPA with the firm J. Walter Thompson. As of March 13, 1996, the firm J. Walter Thompson was not a Section 8(a) concern. The INS COTR who awarded the task orders for the requirement under the BPAs understood that J. Walter Thompson was not a Section 8(a) concern.

In a letter dated May 16, 1996, the INS provided its first written notice to the SBA regarding its intention to procure services for its requirement from non-Section 8(a) concerns. In this same letter, the contracting officer, John Russo, confirmed his belief that the INS was obligated to notify the SBA when the INS decided to satisfy the requirement through non-Section 8(a) contractors:

> Further, because the INS' urgent requirements for advertising remains unfulfilled, the INS will seek to immediately place orders, to meet these requirements, under existing contracts within the Federal Government. It is not our intention to solicit an 8(a) firm from your office to fulfill this requirement. During this period prior to selection of J. Cooper & Associates, numerous 8(a) firms were assessed, with no company possessing the qualifications appropriate for this requirement.

SBA regulation 13 CFR 124 8(a) clearly states: "A decision to terminate a specific 8(a) contract for default can be made by the procuring activity contracting officer after consulting with SBA. The contracting officer must advise SBA of any intent to terminate an 8(a) contract for default in writing before doing so." The INS never provided any written request to the SBA regarding JCA's contract.

The undisputed facts show that the INS requirement was set aside for the Section 8(a) Program, and that INS failed to provide **written notice** to the SBA of its decision in March 1996 to use non-Section 8(a) concerns to satisfy the INS requirement. On these issues, the INS clearly violated the mandate of FAR 19.506(c) (1995). Moreover, this INS violation of FAR 19.506(c), as well as the INS's multiple violations of the FAR provisions governing simplified acquisition procedures, were integral parts of the INS's overall conduct to rid itself of JCA and to evade its contractual duties to JCA. This INS conduct was improper and illegal.

The INS conduct violated both the letter and the spirit of the FAR regulations governing simplified acquisition procedures. One of the purposes of simplified acquisition procedures is to **"improve opportunities for small business and small disadvantaged business concerns to obtain a fair proportion of Government contracts"** (FAR 13.102(b), 1995). In its scheme to avoid JCA, however, the INS used the simplified acquisition procedures to do just the opposite—to deny opportunities to a Section 8(a) business. **Furthermore, the INS use of BPAs violates the FAR's stated purpose of protecting small business set-asides**. FAR 13.204(c) (1995) states that "the existence of a BPA does not justify purchasing from only one source or avoiding small business set-asides."

SBA FAILURE TO ENFORCE
FAR REGULATIONS AND SBA'S POLICIES:

The Small Business Administration Minority Small Business and Capital Ownership Program SOP [Standard Operating Procedures] 80-05-02 ("SBA SOP") impose upon the SBA duties that it must fulfill in favor of Section 8(a) concerns. These duties include the following:

• Providing technical and managerial aids and counseling and assistance to SBA 8(a) concerns and acting as advocate and protecting the interest of 8(a) concerns, and

• Making every effort to ensure that 8(a) concerns are offered contracts at a **"fair market price"** and contracts that will enable the 8(a) concern to make a **"reasonable profit"**.

As will be shown, however, **the SBA failed to fulfill any of these obligations to JCA.**

The SBA's enabling statute imposes upon the SBA the duty to provide technical and managerial assistance to Section 8(a) concerns (such as JCA) as follows:

> *It shall...be the duty of the [SBA]* and it is empowered, whenever it determines such action is necessary...*to provide technical and managerial aids to small business concerns, by advising and counseling on matters in connection with Government procurement* and property disposal and on policies, principles, and practices of good management, including but not limited to cost accounting (15 U.S.C. § 637 (b) (1) (A) (1994)).

The same statute also imposes upon the SBA the duty to ensure that 8(a) concerns receive **"fair and reasonable treatment"** from Federal agencies-such as the INS-with which the SBA and the Section 8(a) concern contract:

> *It shall also be the duty of the [SBA]* and it is empowered, whenever it determines such action is necessary...to consult and cooperate with all Government agencies for the purpose of *ensuring that small-business concerns receive fair and reasonable treatment from such agencies* (15 U.S.C. 637(b) (1) (1994)).

These duties are further underscored in the SBA's implementing regulations, particularly with regard to Section 8(a) concerns. (Relevant SBA implementing regulations are found at 13 C.F.R. Part 101 ("Administration") and 13 C.F.R. Part 124 (Section 8(a) implementing regulations). 13 C.F.R.

124. I (1995) ("Scope of regulations") states that "these regulations [Part 124] implement section [1] 8(a)...of the Small
Business Act [15 U.S.C. 637(a)].") . For example, the SBA regulations provide that it has a duty to aid, counsel, assist, and
protect the interests of the Section 8(a) concerns in their
dealings with federal agencies (13 C.F.R. 101.1 (1995); see
also 15 U.S.C. 631 (1994)).

SBA's regulations impose upon it the duty to ensure that
contracts awarded to Section 8(a) concerns will enable
such concerns to perform the contract and "earn a reasonable profit" (13 C.F.R. 124.307(a), (1995), "Contractual
assistance"). These regulations also provide that the agency issuing the task orders to an 8(a) concern is obligated to
issue them at a "fair market price" (13 C.F.R. 124.315 (1995)).
Additionally, the regulations provide that, when appropriate, the SBA should request that agencies (such as the INS)
demonstrate proof to the SBA, by submission of **written material,** that they have used appropriate methods, such as
commercial prices for similar products, when determining
the "fair market price" (13 C.F.R 124.315 (1995)). The SBA's
implementing regulations state:

(a)   A "fair market price" for an 8(a) contract shall be
determined by the agency offering the requirement to
SBA accordance with paragraphs (a)(1) and (a)(2) of this
section.

(b)   Upon the request of SBA, an agency offering a procurement requirement for potential award through the 8(a)
program shall submit to SBA a written statement detailing
the method used by the agency to estimate the current fair
market price for the contract (13 C.F.R. 124.315 (1995), ("Fair
Market price for 8(a) awards"). See also SBA SOP 99(j), pp.
263–265).

In fact, the SBA contracting officer acknowledged that, pursuant to these provisions, the SBA would ask an agency to provide the basis for its estimate of the fair market price of services in the event that the cost or price of an item became a "major issue" under the SBA contract. **INS could not provide an agency's estimate of the fair market price analysis. The SBA did not follow any of the above regulations in dealing with the JCA/INS contract. The SBA played a passive role and thus helped to destroy JCA.**

CONCLUSION—FAR FACTS:

The U.S. Federal Claims Court was given all the above FAR references to consider. The Court was *silent*. **No matter what,** if a contract is an IDIQ contract, requirements contract, or any type of contract, the FAR Regulations must be applied. The INS contracting officers, the SBA contracting officers, and the courts were fully aware that these FAR regulations were never implemented in the JCA-/INS contract. Clearly, the law was ignored by the courts.

It's Still Going On Today

One of the fundamental issues with my case was how the SBA was party to a tripartite contract, where undisputed facts demonstrate that the SBA absolutely failed to fulfill its statutory and contractual duties to JCA as a Section 8(a) contractor. SBA was obligated to serve as an advisor and counselor to JCA and the INS. The SBA in this case, for a period of over three full months, unreasonably and inexplicably ignored JCA's repeated pleas for guidance and assistance.

Many government investigations and private studies conducted since 2003 have verified that hundreds of government contracts set aside for small businesses have instead been awarded to Fortune 500 corporations claiming to be small businesses. They are awarded over $135 billion a year. As far back as I can remember the SBA has attempted to justify the diversion of billions in small business contracts to Fortune 500 firms as "miscoding." This includes small business contracts to Italian defense giant Finmeccanica, Lockheed Martin, Raytheon, Citigroup, Walmart, Rolls Royce, British Aerospace (BAE), General Electric, and Ssangyong from South Korea. In 2006 the SBA issued a press release, claiming the diversion of federal small business contracts to large firms was a "myth." During this same period, Karen Hontz, the SBA's associate administrator for government contracting, stated, "we're looking into…miscoding discrepancies. We will have an explanation, but it takes time." Five years later the fraudulent activities committed by large government contractors are still going on.

The Small Business Act of 1953 mandates that every year, the federal government must give 23 percent of the total value of all federal prime contracts to small businesses. According to ASBL statistics from the SBA Office of Advocacy, small businesses make up more than 56 percent of the U.S. economy, provide 75 percent of the net new jobs added to the economy, represent 99.7 percent of all employers, employ 50.7 percent of the private workforce, provide 40.9 percent of private sales in the country, and represent 97 percent of all U.S. exporters. This is even despite the billions each year in federal "small business" contracts that are instead given to large and international corporations being counted toward the federal small business procurement goal. Small businesses across the nation are losing contracts due to large corporations fraudulently misrepresenting themselves as small businesses.

Legislative and Executive
Branches of Government Fail to Act

In recent years the legislative branch of government has held numerous hearings on the problem of small business contracts going to large businesses representing themselves as small businesses. These hearings claim to look at how congressional oversight has failed and how regulatory loopholes allow large businesses to get and keep small business contracts. However, despite the hearings, the problem still exists.

Senator John F. Kerry, D-Mass, former Chairman of the Committee on Small Business and Entrepreneurship, had "proposed giving SBA more time to complete size determinations to help prevent big businesses from slipping under the radar of a bureaucratic contracting process." (NY TIMES 12/06). The SBA requires businesses to report their size every five years. Senator Kerry's proposal would require annual reports.

On June 30, 2007, an SBA rule change mandated that all firms receiving federal small business contracts must recertify their small business status every five years. However, companies that had contracts in place prior to June 30th, 2007, are only required to recertify that status every twenty years. Through this loophole, large firms were able to acquire small companies with long-term ten- to twenty-year small business contracts and maintain these contracts through that recertification period. It is estimated that through this "grandfather" policy, from 2007 to 2012, more than $300 billion will have been diverted from legitimate small businesses to some of the largest companies in the United States and Europe.

I spent a lot of time writing to Congresswoman Nydia M. Velazquez, D-NY, and former chairwoman of the House Small Business Committee. She stated in a NY Times article dated December 27, 2006, that she would "work to rectify the problems faced by Mr. Cooper and other small businesses by ensuring that there is an effective protest system in place." She also stated that she wants "to make sure that penalties are in place." On August 16, 2006, she stated, "What we are seeing is a sheer lack of accountability from the administration that is resulting in these large businesses receiving Small Business Awards." She further stated, "As a consequence, entrepreneurs are getting less and less contracting opportunities each year." It's ironic, but the same problems still exist today.

Federal laws provide many avenues that are supposed to help small businesses to protest when it comes to contract procedures in which the contractor alleges government wrong doing. In my opinion, the regulations and policies place an impossible standard for the small business to misrepresent its small business status. In my numerous letters to Senator Kerry and Congresswoman Velazquez, I went to great lengths to explain how easy it was for J. Walter Thompson, Bernard Hodes, and CASS Communications violated the Business Opportunity Development Reform Act of 1988 (Public Law 100-656). I explained in great detail how these contractors signed government orders, representing themselves to be "disadvantaged" businesses when they were not, and how the INS and SBA were fully aware of these facts and did nothing to help JCA.

Their representations, to the contrary, were fraud against the United States. As a result of their fraud, these contractors received orders for advertising and public relations support services from the INS. They presented claims for payment and were paid for services rendered. These acts were violations of 31 U.S.C. 3729(a) (1), (2), and (3).

I believe some type of reprimand should have been directed toward the INS, for enabling these contractors to lie on government forms, and toward the SBA, for turning a blind eye to these activities. I have long felt that some reprimand should have been issued by the courts toward the DOJ IG Office, which conducted an investigation that confirmed these contractors had lied on government forms, misrepresenting their small business status, and that the INS was aware of these illegal activities—yet nothing was done to correct the problem. Charles T. Huggins, the agent in charge of conducting the investigations, did nothing with his findings. I have no insight into the motivations of the Justice Department officials who were responsible for investigating the INS's actions. I can only suggest that at that time, the INS was a subordinate service under the Department of Justice, which placed the DOJ officials in the position of investigating misconduct in its own house.

Change Is Necessary

Through my many years of dealing with members of Congress, my elected officials, and numerous administration officials concerning my case, I can honestly say there is an arrogant attitude of power and insensitivity toward small businesses among many elected officials, contracting officers, and program staffers. Many government workers throughout the SBA, INS, and the Justice Department were not responsive to my needs. They feel that they can do whatever they please, and they are rude.

I have witnessed this attitude—that "you are unimportant because you can't do anything for me, and you haven't any power base." They talk down to small business owners as if they are stupid; and most of all, they refuse to be accountable in their failure to enforce the law. It seems to me that many government workers within these agencies today do not realize that they work for the people, not for themselves or special-interest groups.

The issue of how the federal government spends the contract money it sets aside for small businesses is critical not only to small businesses but also to the communities in which those small businesses are located. Often, those communities have many small businesses with fewer than twenty employees. These small businesses can be the lifeblood of the communities and their economy. It is important that small businesses get the contracts that are set aside for them.

My hope is that the true story that I have reveal in this book will shed light on how the SBA's contracting program for SDB and set-aside programs work and point out the difficulties small businesses have obtaining truth and justice, particularly when they have to go through the court system. To this day SBA refuses to explain why they failed to implement the Business Opportunity Reform Act of 1988 (P.L. 100-656), and the SBA IG refused to explain why his office has rejected to investigate JCA complaints. They are conceited, it is call take what we say or forget it. We are accountable to nobody.

With a bit of luck, my story will help small businesses, contract lawyers with small business clients, future small business owners, and the general public take a step forward on the path of understanding and help fight to correct the flaws in our federal government's small business contracting program. Small businesses across the nation are losing the fight for contracts intended for legitimate small and minority-owned businesses as a result of large companies fraudulently misrepresenting themselves as small, disadvantaged businesses. In Report 5-15 the SBA IG described the abuse as "one of the most important challenges facing the SBA and the entire federal government today."

It is not an easy or inexpensive process to enter the 8(a) certification program. It takes a great deal of time, work, and money. JCA did nothing wrong; JCA was performing its contract and was working in good faith with the INS and SBA. However, the INS and SBA were not working in good faith with JCA. The SBA should have protected JCA instead of participating with the INS's wrongdoing.

COOPER'S FINAL
THOUGHTS

The letter contract executed by JCA, the SBA, and the INS created express obligations as well as implied duties to cooperate and not to hinder performance. Notwithstanding these obligations, and as described in detail above, the INS failed to pay invoices, issued work to other contractors (some of which were not "small businesses"), failed to issue written task orders, and failed to negotiate task orders for a reasonable price. And despite the SBA's knowledge of the INS's behavior and JCA's repeated requests for assistance, the SBA failed to take any action to assist JCA to resolve these issues during contract performance.

No matter how one evaluates the facts and evidence of this case, J. Walter Thompson, Bernard Hodes, and Cass Communications lied on government orders, representing themselves as disadvantaged businesses when, in fact, they were not. They took this action with the INS's cooperation to acquire the government contract set-aside for JCA as an SBA 8(a) contractor. Laws were broken, and JCA went out of business.

There is no question in my mind that politics played a part in the way SBA treated JCA. SBA's only concern should have been to protect its 8(a) contractor and see that it was treated fairly by the INS. Instead, SBA was apparently more concerned with protecting special-interest group companies J. Walter Thompson, Bernard Hodes, and CASS Communications. To accomplish this objective, SBA lied, misrepresented the truth, and failed to enforce the law. There was no accountability to make ensure that the SBA followed the law and do its job. SBA clearly makes its own laws and ignores congressional laws as it sees fit. I did not enter the SBA program to go out of business, but that's what happened.

Well, that's my story. I hope I have provided information about a very troubling and serious issue that small businesses still face today. As I mentioned earlier, I trust the information in this book is helpful to small business owners, future small business owners, and the general public.

I have often wondered over the years how things might have turned out if the SBA had done its job and enforced the law. Would I still be in business? Where did I go wrong to allow the INS and SBA to destroy my business? How could I have done things differently?

President Obama recognized the magnitude of the issue, stating, "It is time to end the diversion of small business contracts to corporate giants." I read his words and smiled. I am sad to say I'm not optimistic, but I'm hopeful.

TABLE OF AUTHORITIES

COURT CASES

A & S Council Oil Co. v. Saiki, 799 F. Supp. 1221 (D.D.C. 1992), rev'd on other grounds, 56 F.3d 234 (D.C.Cir. 1995).

A-Transport Northwest Co. v. United States, 27 Fed. Cl. 206 (1992), aff'd, 36 F.3d 1576 (Fed. Cir. 1994).

Allenfield Associates v. United States, 40 Fed. Cl. 471 (1998).

AT&T Technologies, Inc. v. United States, 18 Cl. Ct. 315 (1989).

Brooklyn & Queens Screen Manufacturing Co. v. United States, 97 Ct. Cl. 532 (194).

Celeron Gathering Corp. v. United States, 34 Fed. Cl. 745 (1996).

Ceredo Mortuary Chapel v. United States, 29 Fed. Cl. 346 (1993).

Crown Laundry & Dry Cleaners, Inc. v, United States, 29 Fed. Cl. 506 (1993).

Darwin Construction Co. v. United States, 811 F. 2d 593 (Fed. Cir. 1987).

Davies Precision Machining, Inc. v. United States, 35 Fed. Cl. 651 (1996).

Dubinsky v. United States, 43 Fed. Cl. 243 (1999).

George A. Fuller Co. v. United States, 108 Ct. Cl. 70, 69 F. Supp. 409 (1947).

Malone v. United States, 849 F.2d 1441 (Fed. Cir. 1988), *modified on other grounds,* 857 F.2d 787 (Fed. Cir. 1988).

Mapco Alaska Petroleum, Inc. v. United States, 27 Fed. Cl. 405 (1992).

Northern Helex Co. v. United States, 197 Ct. Cl. 118, 455 F. 2d 546 (1972).

O'Neill v. United States, 231 Ct. Cl. 823 (1982).

Smith v. United States, 34 Fed. Cl. 313 (1995), *appeal dismissed,* 91 F.3d 165 (Fed. Cir. 1996). ..

Suburban Contracting Co. v. United States, 76 Ct. Cls. 533 (1932).

Torncello v. United States, 231 Ct. Cl. 20, 681 F.2d 756 (1982).

Wells Fargo Bank, N.A. v. United States, 33 Fed. Cl. 233 (1995), rev'd in part on other grounds, 88 F. 3d 1012 (Fed. Cir. 1996), cert. den'd, 520 U.S. 1116 (1997).

AGENCY BOARD CASES

Adams Manufacturing Co., GSBCA No. 5747, 82-1 B.C.A.

Doris A. Lahage, GSBCA No. 7321, 84-2 B.C.A.

Johnson & Son Erectors Co., ASBCA Nos. 23689, 24564, 81-1 B.C.A.

Laboratory for Electronics, Inc. ASBCA No. 13019, 69-2 B.C.A.

Nexus Construction Co., ASBCA No. 31070, 92-2 B.C.A.

28 TEM Associates, Inc., DOT BCA No. 2024, 89-1 BCA

STATUTES, RULES AND REGULATIONS

15 U.S.C. § 631 (1994).

U.S.C. § 637(a).

15 U.S.C. § 637(b) (1)(A) (1994).

13 C.F.R. § 101.1 (1995).

13 C.F.R. § 124.1 (1995).

13 C.F.R. § 124.100 (1995).

13 C.F.R. § 124.307(a) (1995).

13 C.F.R. § 124.315 (1995).

48 C.F.R. § 13.101 (1995).

48 C.F.R. § 13.102 (1995).

48 C.F.R. § 13.103 (1995).

48 C.F.R. § 13.204 (1995).

48 C.F.R. § 16.505 (1994).

48 C.F.R. § 16.506 (1999).

48 C.F.R. § 19.506 (1995).

48 C.F.R. § 32.905 (1995).

MISCELLANEOUS

Restatement (Second) of Contracts § 205 (1981).

Restatement (Second) of Contracts § 235(2) (1981).

SBA SOP 99(j), pp. 263–65

RESOURCE

NY Times

American Small Business League

The CASE is a book based on facts and the author's knowledge of the issues. The exact argument made before the U.S. Court of Federal Claims is presented.

SUPPORTING
DOCUMENTATION

1. John A. Russo, Jr., INS contracting officer letter to Shapleigh Drisco, SBA dated. May 16, 1996. This letter confirms the fact that INS had to notify SBA before Executing any modification to the INS JCA contract

U.S. Department of Justice
Immigration and Naturalization Service

425 I Street NW.
Washington, DC 20536

MAY 16 1996

Mr. Shapleigh Drisco
U.S. Small Business Administration
1110 Vermont Avenue, N.W.
Washington, D.C. 20043

    Subject: Letter Contract COW-5-C-0017, J. Cooper & Associates, Inc.

Dear Mr. Drisco:

    As you are aware, the Immigration and Naturalization Service (INS) has been pursuing the definitization of subject contract, awarded on July 25, 1995, under the 8(a) Program. In order to definitize, the Defense Contract Audit Agency (DCAA) required documentation from the contractor, which the contractor only recently provided. This lack of definitization has greatly impacted the advertising program which is an important, high priority requirement at the INS.

    There have been numerous, unsuccessful attempts by DCAA to conduct an assist audit to determine the adequacy of the contractor's accounting system. The DCAA concluded in December 1995, that the contractor's accounting system was inadequate. The contractor has continued to make corrections to its system in an attempt to support costs that were incurred.

    Because of the difficulties experienced in obtaining this information and our resultant inability to fully pay invoices, the contractor has become very frustrated and recently requested that we terminate the contract for convenience. Conversely, the program office believes the contractor has not delivered quality products and services, requesting a termination for default. It has become clear that continuing a contractual relationship with this contractor is not beneficial to either party. In addition, the contractor has priced prospective INS requirements outside the realm of reasonableness and affordability from this agency's perspective. Consequently, INS has concluded that pursuing definitization, and/or continuing performance under this contract, in light of these issues, would not be in the best interest of either party.

INS 0425

00000363

Page 2
Shapleigh Drisco

The proposed course of action for final and complete resolution of the problems between INS and Cooper, is to allow the agreement to lapse and request the contractor to prepare a proposal for costs incurred in the performance of the contract. We anticipate a negotiated settlement of reasonable, allowable, and allocable costs for work performed under task orders. Support of this strategy is requested from Small Business Administration as a reasonable alternative to termination.

Further, because the INS' urgent requirements for advertising remains unfulfilled, the INS will seek to immediately place orders, to meet these requirements, under existing contracts within the Federal Government. It is not our intention to solicit an 8(a) firm from your office to fulfill this requirement. During the period prior to selection of J. Cooper & Associates, numerous 8(a) firms were assessed, with no company possessing the qualifications appropriate for this requirement.

I can assure you the INS has a strong commitment to the Small Business Administration initiatives and the support that is given to its programs. However, in light of the protracted issues that remain unresolved with this contractor, it is incumbent upon this office to take this action and to provide immediate support of this important program.

Sincerely,

John A. Russo, Jr.
Contracting Officer

HQPRO:AGRIMSLEY:SDRISCO:LP:5/16/96
OFFICIAL FILE
READING
HQADM

2. Blanket Purchasing Agreement dated 03/22/96, amount $25,000 signed by Lesa P. Scott, INS contracting officer. It shows J. Walter Thompson, claiming to be a Disadvantaged small business on government documentation

....DER FOR SUPPLIES OR SERVICES				PAGE 1	OF	PAGES 2

IMPORTANT: Mark all packages and papers with contract and/or order numbers.

1. TE OF ORDER	2. CONTRACT NO. (if any)	3. ORDER NO.	4. REQUISITION/REFERENCE NO.
11/13/96		COW-6-P-0384	BOR-6-00091

ING OFFICE (Address correspondence to)
Immigration & Naturalization Svc
Headquarters Procurement
I Street, N.W., Room 2208
Washington, D.C. 20536

6. SHIP TO: (Consignee and address, ZIP Code)
N/A

SHIP VIA:

CONTRACTOR (Name, address and ZIP Code)

J. WALTER THOMPSON
ATN: BECKY
56 FIFTEENTH ST NW
WASHINGTON, DC 20005

8. TYPE OF ORDER

[X] A. PURCHASE - Reference your ____

Please furnish the following on the terms and conditions specified on both sides of this order and on the attached sheets, if any, including delivery as indicated. This purchase is negotiated under authority of:

[ ] B. DELIVERY - Except for billing instructions on the reverse, this delivery order is subject to instructions contained on this side only of this form and is issued subject to the terms and conditions of the above-numbered contract.

ACCOUNTING AND APPROPRIATIONS DATA
1217/61HR.537B.000.96

10. REQUISITIONING OFFICE
HQBOR, ROOM 7232

11. BUSINESS CLASSIFICATION (Check appropriate box(es))
[ ] SMALL [ ] OTHER THAN SMALL [X] DIS-ADVANTAGED [ ] WOMEN-OWNED

B. POINT estination	14. GOVERNMENT B/L NO.	15. DELIVER TO F.O.B. POINT ON OR BEFORE (Date) 03/22/96	16. DISCOUNT TERMS Net 30 Days

ACE OF INSPECTION AND ACCEPTANCE
tination

17. SCHEDULE (See reverse for Rejections)						
NO.	SUPPLIES OR SERVICES (B)	QUANTITY ORDERED (C)	UNIT (D)	UNIT PRICE (E)	AMOUNT (F)	QUANTITY ACCEPTED (G)
	******CONFIRMING VERBAL******					
	CLASSIFIED ADS FOR RECRUITMENT OF BORDER PATROL AGENTS.	1	EA	$25000.00	$25000.00	
	INS POINT OF CONTACT: ELLIE MILLER RM 2038 202/514-0844					
	QUESTION REGARDING PAYMENT PLEASE CALL OUR FINANCE BRANCH AT 202/616-7742.					

18. SHIPPING POINT LING	19. GROSS SHIPPING WEIGHT	20. INVOICE NO.	17(H). TOT. Cont pages $0.00

21. MAIL INVOICE TO: (Include ZIP Code)
US IMMIGRATION & NATZ. SERVICE FINANCE BRANCH
425 I STREET, N.W., ROOM 4007 WASHINGTON, D.C. 20536

17.(I). GRAND TOTAL $25000.00

ITED STATES OF AMERICA
BY (Signature)
40-01-152-8083

23. NAME (Typed)
LESA P. SCOTT
TITLE: CONTRACTING/ORDERING OFFICER
50347-101

OPTIONAL FORM 347 (10-83)
Prescribed by GSA; FAR (48 CFR) 53.213(e)

3. Blanket Purchasing Agreement dated 11/13/95, amount $7,062.15 signed by Betty Johnson, INS contracting officer. It confirms CASS Recruitment Publications. Stating they are disadvantaged small business on government documentation

ORDER FOR SUPPLIES OR SERVICES

IMPORTANT: Mark all packages and papers with contract and/or order numbers.

			PAGE	OF	PAGES
			1		3

1. DATE OF ORDER	2. CONTRACT NO. (If any)	3. ORDER NO.	4. REQUISITION/REFERENCE NO.
11/13/95		COW-6-P-0131	BOR-6-00016

5. ISSUING OFFICE (Address correspondence to)
IMMIGRATION & NATZ. SERVICE
CONTRACTING & PROCUREMENT BRANCH
425 I ST., N.W., ROOM 2102
WASHINGTON, D.C. 20536

6. SHIP TO: (Consignee and address, ZIP Code)
SEE ATTACHED PAGE

SHIP VIA:

7. TO: CONTRACTOR (Name, address and ZIP Code)
CASS RECRUITMENT PUBLICATIONS
ATTN: DIANE ANDERSON
369 LEXINTON AVENUE
NEW YORK, NY 10017-6506

8. TYPE OF ORDER
[X] A. PURCHASE - Reference your _____
Please furnish the following on the terms and conditions specified on both sides of this order and on the attached sheets, if any, including delivery as indicated. This purchase is negotiated under authority of:

[ ] B. DELIVERY - Except for billing instructions on the reverse, this delivery order is subject to instructions contained on this side only of this form and is issued subject to the terms and conditions of the above-numbered contract.

9. ACCOUNTING AND APPROPRIATIONS DATA
156121761HR537B000

10. REQUISITIONING OFFICE
HQBOR, ROOM 7232

11. BUSINESS CLASSIFICATION (Check appropriate box(es))
[ ] SMALL [ ] OTHER THAN SMALL [X] DIS-ADVAN-TAGED [ ] WOMEN-OWNED

12. F.O.B. POINT	14. GOVERNMENT B/L NO.	15. DELIVER TO F.O.B. POINT ON OR BEFORE (Date)	16. DISCOUNT TERMS
Destination		11/13/95	Net 30 Days

13. PLACE OF INSPECTION AND ACCEPTANCE
Destination

17. SCHEDULE (See reverse for Rejections)

ITEM NO. (A)	SUPPLIES OR SERVICES (B)	QUANTITY ORDERED (C)	UNIT (D)	UNIT PRICE (E)	AMOUNT (F)	QUANTITY ACCEPTED (G)
	THE CONTRACTOR SHALL SUPPLY THE FOLLOWING					
1	NEWSPAPER ADS TO BE PLACED IN THE GEORGIA COLLEGE AND MILITARY NEWSPAPERS TO ADVERTISE FOR TARGETED RECRUITMENT OF BORDER PATROL AGENT TRAINEE POSITIONS	1	SR	$7062.15	$7062.15	
	COLLEGE 1 AT $3811.70 COLLEGE 2 AT $2082.75 MILITARY 1 AT $1167.70					
	TOTAL COST $7062.15					
	SEE ATTACHED					
	INS POINT OF CONTACT IS ELLIE MILLER ROOM 2038 202/514-0844					
	(continued)				INS 1152	

18. SHIPPING POINT	19. GROSS SHIPPING WEIGHT	20. INVOICE NO.	17(H). TOT.
SEE BILLING INSTRUCTIONS ON REVERSE			$0.00 Cont pages

21. MAIL INVOICE TO: (Include ZIP Code)
US IMMIGRATION & NATZ. SERVICE FINANCE BRANCH
425 I STREET, N.W., ROOM 4007 WASHINGTON, D.C. 20536

17. (J). GRAND TOTAL $7062.15

22. UNITED STATES OF AMERICA
BY (Signature)

23. NAME (Typed)
BETTY JOHNSON
TITLE: CONTRACTING/ORDERING OFFICER

NSN 7540-01-152-6083
FILE

50347-101

OPTIONAL FORM 347 (10-83)
Prescribed by GSA; FAR (48 CFR) 53.213(e)

FROM : CO CASS COMMUNICATIONS   708 475 8807 TO 912825144288   P.82/12

INVOICE

CASS COMMUNICATIONS, INC.

Procurement

Tel 708 475.1800
Fax 708 475.1807

PLEASE REMIT TO:
CASS COMMUNICATIONS, INC.
P.O. BOX 71545
CHICAGO, IL 60694

INVOICE #: 143117

 # 143117

December 19, 1995

Evanton, IV   847-733-9370
847-733-9100

ATTN: MS. ELLIE MILLER
US DEPT OF IMMIGRATION &
NATURALIZATION
425 I STREET, NW
WASHINGTON, DC 20536

COW-6-P-0131

RE: US DEPT/IMMIGRATION AND NAT.
Your order #: COW-6-P-0131 COLLEGE

COW-6-P-0132   -0000T

This invoice reflects the amount due for advertising as referenced above. Questions may be
referred to our Accounts Receivable Dept., at (708) 475-8800. Thank you for your order.

INVOICE SUMMARY

Amount Due......................... $4,356.85

Payment is due by January 19, 1996.

THIS INVOICE COVERS TEARSHEETS RECEIVED TO DATE FOR YOUR ORDER.

ADDITIONAL INVOICING TO FOLLOW.

RATES SHOWN ARE NET/NET.

THANK YOU.

Please pay promptly
Services Rendered
E. Miller
3/25/96

TERMS: NET 30 DAYS. A late penalty of 1.75% per month, or the maximum amount allowed under state law, will be charged to past
due invoices. Any discrepancies must be reported to us within 15 days of invoice date.

Accounting Copy   *Payne, Denise C.*   *Amy Silver*

INS 1160

00000432

4. Michelle Wall, INS contracting officer letter dated July 7, 1995 to SBA, Patricia Collins requesting permission to negotiate INS Letter Contract with JCA

U.S. Departmen. .f Justice   P.6

Immigration and Naturalization Service

Exhibit I

425 Eye Street N.W.
Washington. D.C. 20536

July 7, 1995

0353-95-0844
agency 11601
Case # 32842

U.S. Small Business Administration
Washington District Office
ATTN: Patricia Collins, Business Opportunity Specialist
1110 Vermont Avenue, N.W., 9th Floor
Washington, D.C. 20043

Dear Ms. Collins:

The Immigration and Naturalization Service (INS) has an immediate requirement for the services of a firm to provide public relations and advertising services in support of our Immigration Officer Recruitment Campaign by designing advertising campaigns for recruitment purposes, producing recruitment videos, designing and placing newspaper and magazine advertisements, designing brochures and posters, and creating recruiting exhibits. A draft statement of work is enclosed for your perusal.

In accordance with 8(a) procedures for the procurement of supplies, services, and research and development requirements, the following information is furnished:

a.	Government estimate:	$1,600,000/annually, $8 million total with a minimum guarantee of $250,000 in the base year
b.	Procurement history:	This is a new requirement
c.	Period of performance:	Twelve (12) months with four (4) option periods
d.	SIC Code:	The SIC code for this requirement is 8743 - Public Relations Services with a size standard of $3.5 million
e.	Special requirements:	Security clearances (level TBD)

This office requests permission to negotiate an indefinite delivery, indefinite quantity contract directly with J. Cooper and Associates, Inc., an 8(a) certified firm located at 1900 L. Street, N.W., Suite 706, Washington, D.C., 20036. Public solicitations for this requirement have not been issued.

000048

103

Page 2

     Due to the urgency of this requirement, a separate letter contract request is accompaning this letter. Please confirm the proposed firm's eligibility under the 8(a) program and their SIC code certification. If approved, please advise this office of the SBA contract number to be assigned to this proposed acquisition. A response is requested by July 17 to coincide with the letter contract approval date. Thank you for your attention to this urgent matter.

     Refer any questions to the undersigned at 202/514-3258.

Sincerely,

3353 FAX

Michelle Wall
Contracting Officer

enclosure

000049

00000147

5. Department of Justice Memorandum of Investigation dated July 15, 1997. It confirms INS knew that J. Walter Thompson, CASS Recruitment Publications and Bernard Hodes verified their small and disadvantaged business status to the INS Both the DOJ IG and the SBA IG knew from the investigative report that the contractors violated numerous SBA regulations along with the Business Opportunity Reform Act of 1988 (P.L. 100-656)

U.S. Department of Justice
Office of the Inspector General

MEMORANDUM OF INVESTIGATION

Case Number:	Reporting Office:
# 9701350	Washington Field Office

RE: Interview of ██████████

06546

On July 15, 1997, ████████ met with Immigration and Naturalization Service (INS) █████████████████████████ at 425 I Street, Washington, D.C. 20536, to discuss allegations that certain businesses had received "small business" status, when these companies did not meet the requirements as "small businesses."

██████ advised ████████ that in January 1996, she switched places with ████████████ in Small Procurement and then ████████ filled her position in the Automated Data Processing (ADP) Unit as a Contracting Officer. ████ said that with this switch, she inherited certain standing files from ███████████ such as the advertising companies-Blanket Purchase Agreements (BPAs). ████████ explained that under the Federal Acquisition Regulations (FAR), small procurement, is governed by the Simplified Acquisition Procedures, (FAR-13),(copy attached to memorandum). She explained that a BPA is a type of "charge account" with minimal payment terms. When an order is placed, one will get prices confirmed and compare these to other vendors for competition or to merely rotate the work among the vendors. ████████ stated that in January 1996, the regulations were amended and now a BPA can have a "ceiling", the amount of money that can be paid out in a year's time frame, to $100,000.00 instead of the former $25,000.00 amount.

████████ stated that in November 1995, the INS engaged in a large recruiting effort to hire large numbers of entry level employees. She stated that different advertising companies were then called upon to facilitate this effort of recruiting for the INS. ████████ explained that there was initially an existing contract in place with J. Cooper & Associates for such advertising, however this was not a "requirements contract" and so multiple vendors could still be utilized for the INS advertising campaign if INS desired to employ other companies. On the other hand, if the contract was a "requirements contracts" than J. Cooper & Associates would have exclusive rights to this advertising campaign. ████████ believed that INS decided to use other vendors because they were not happy with J. Cooper & Associates performance and so BPAs were established for other advertising companies. She said that her Supervisor, ████████ would know more about the poor performance situation of the company. ████████ could not recall who advised her of this unfavorable situation with J. Cooper & Associates.

████████ explained that normal FAR procedures allow verbal verification of a company's "small business" status over the phone for simplified contracts. However, a Contracting Specialist also has the discretion

Special Agent Name and Signature:		Date:	July 15, 1997

OIG Form III-107/1 (10/23/96) This document contains neither recommendations nor conclusions of the IG. It is the property of the IG and is loaned to your agency; it and its contents are not to be distributed outside of your agency.

to send formal paperwork for "small business" certification for more complex orders. ▓▓▓▓▓said that BPAs can be established for years, but must be reviewed annually to see if the services are still required by INS or the company. She stated that these advertising BPAs were not renewed because their services were no longer needed for 1997 Fiscal Year. ▓▓▓▓▓ believed that instead an Inter-Agency agreement was put into place by▓▓▓▓▓▓▓▓in INS Programs for INS advertising needs.

▓▓▓▓▓ stated that the vendors involved with the advertising campaign, Abramson, Ehrlich & Manes, Cass Recruitment Publications, Bernard Hodes and Thompson Recruitment (also known as J. Walter Thompson & J.W.T. Specialized Communications), verified their "small business" status verbally with▓▓▓▓▓▓▓as noted in the file. She explained that under the FAR, Small Business Programs, Part 19, Major Group 73, Business Services, (copy attached to memorandum) each company had to be under a five million dollar cap to qualify as a "small business." ▓▓▓▓ believed that each company was truthful in claiming their status as such and had no reason to doubt their certifications. She provided SA▓▓▓▓with copies of each company's BPA folder for her review.

06547

106

6. NY Times Article "Small Businesses Fight Fickle Rules

The New York Times

Small Businesses Fight Fickle Rules

By RON NIXON

Published: December 27, 2006

In 1995, Joseph N. Cooper won a multiyear contract worth up to $8 million to do public relations for the Immigration and Naturalization Service. He received the contract through a Small Business Administration program established to increase opportunities for small companies.

But not long after the work was under way, the deal was awarded instead to three multimillion-dollar companies, which were listed as disadvantaged in contract documents. After years of trying to win the contract back, Mr. Cooper filed a false-claims lawsuit against the companies, asserting that they had committed fraud by saying they were small businesses.

This year, to Mr. Cooper and his lawyer's surprise, the court ruled that although evidence showed the companies were indeed not small businesses, fraud had not been committed because the I.N.S. knew their true status when the work was awarded to the companies -- J. Walter Thompson, the Bernard Hodes Group and Cass Communications.

The case was dismissed.

"We were floored," Mr. Cooper said in an interview. "The ruling essentially said that I was right, the companies were not small, but so what."

That experience points to the kind of Catch-22 world that some small-business owners face when they challenge the awarding of government contracts.

Many studies have shown that hundreds of government contracts set aside for small business are being awarded to large corporations. Federal laws provide several mechanisms that allow small-business owners who suspect that contracts have been awarded to large companies to protest.

But small-business owners say that the rules in many cases impose nearly impossible standards on them. Even if they do succeed in protesting an award, they say, and prove that federal agencies are intentionally awarding small-business contracts to big companies, there are almost no penalties. Often, the large companies get to keep the contacts.

"It's a hollow victory," said Raul Espinosa, a small-business owner in Florida who has won several protests. "You might win the size protest, but you can't claim the contract because the agency allowed delivery to take place and what's worse, the penalties for the violations aren't enforced."

Mr. Espinosa is leading a coalition of six small-business associations seeking to change the process.

Congress may be more receptive to their calls for change next year, when two longtime critics of the practice assume leadership positions for the committees overseeing small business.

Senator John F. Kerry, Democrat of Massachusetts and the incoming chairman of the Committee on Small Business and Entrepreneurship, has proposed giving the S.B.A. more time to complete size determinations and to help prevent big businesses from slipping under the radar of a bureaucratic contracting process.

The S.B.A. recently required businesses to report their size every five years. Mr. Kerry's proposal would make the reports annual.

"The protest process is supposed to keep the system honest, but what's the point of protesting a contract if nothing happens?" Senator Kerry said

Nydia M. Velázquez, Democrat of New York and the incoming chairwoman of the House Small Business Committee, said she would work to rectify the problems faced by Mr. Cooper and other small businesses by ensuring that there is an effective protest system in place. She also wants to make sure that penalties are enforced.

"The fact that large businesses are being awarded with small-business contracts, and that there is no system in place with penalties or consequences for this, is extremely concerning," Ms. Velázquez said.

If a small-business owner believes that a company has been illegally awarded a small-business contract the owner has several options in protesting the award.

The first is to file a so-called size protest with the S.B.A., asserting that the competitor is too big.

Under this process, a company has five days after being notified of a winning bidder to initiate the protest. If the agency decides that the winning company is not small, it can recommend that the contract be rescinded.

But that almost never happens, Mr. Espinosa says.

Last year, Mr. Espinosa protested an Air Force contract, offering documentation showing that the winning company was actually a subsidiary of a larger concern, and thus ineligible.

At first, the S.B.A. ruled that the company was a small business, but Mr. Espinosa appealed the decision to the agency's Office of Hearings and Appeals and an administrative law judge ruled in his favor. Despite the ruling, the winner kept the contract.

"There needs to be some reform in the size protest system," Mr. Espinosa said. "Otherwise, why should small-business owners bother and why would large companies worry about getting caught?"

The S.B.A. said it could only recommend that contracts be rescinded and could not compel other agencies to follow the recommendation.

Albert B. Krachman, a lawyer at the firm of Blank Rome in Washington, who has represented small businesses, said, "The system is basically set up in such a way that the policing is left up to the businesses themselves."

What's more, he said, "There is no incentive from the contracting officers or other government officials to see if the companies they are giving small business set-asides to are indeed small-business concerns."

Gary M. Jackson, assistant administrator for size standards at the S.B.A., agrees that the policing of the small-business contracting system is left up to competitors, but asserts that they are in a better position than contracting officers to know which is a small business and which is not. Another remedy for small businesses is through the courts.

As Mr. Cooper did, small-business owners can file lawsuits asserting that fraud was committed in the awarding of set-aside contracts to large businesses. But legal specialists say the filing false-claims lawsuits can be a costly undertaking. The law also contains several legal hurdles that make it almost impossible to win, they say.

Mr. Cooper said that he was convinced that a lawsuit was his only hope.

At first, Mr. Cooper and his lawyer argued in the Court of Federal Claims that the I.N.S. had not operated in good faith when it stopped giving him work on the contract.

The I.N.S. said it was not satisfied with Mr. Cooper's work and the cost associated with it. But in a deposition, a contacting officer at the agency said no evidence was ever offered to him questioning the quality of Mr. Cooper's work. A government audit found that the cost was actually reasonable.

Still, the court sided with the I.N.S. and said that because the agency had given Mr. Cooper the minimum amount on the contract there was no evidence the agency had not operated in good faith. Mr. Cooper appealed the ruling, but an appeals court upheld the lower court ruling.

Mr. Cooper and his lawyer then filed a lawsuit in the Federal District Court for the District of Columbia. They argued that the two companies that had been awarded contracts to complete the work that Mr. Cooper's firm had originally been awarded had committed fraud when they said that they were disadvantaged businesses.

A lawyer for the companies, Bruce M. Ginsberg of the law firm of Davis and Gilbert in New York, denies that they ever misstated their size to the I.N.S. "These are multimillion-dollar companies," Mr. Ginsberg said. "They would not represent themselves as small businesses. We have no idea how they came to be marked that way in the I.N.S. documents."

Among the evidence offered by Mr. Cooper were contract documents in which the companies were described as disadvantaged and a Justice Department investigative report showing that the companies had verbally confirmed their disadvantaged status with an officer at the I.N.S., though both companies were two of the largest advertising firms in the country.

"We thought we had a slam-dunk," said Cyrus Phillips, a lawyer doing pro bono work for Mr. Cooper.

But when the judge ruled otherwise, he not only dismissed the case but also ordered Mr. Cooper to pay legal fees and other expenses to the companies he had sued.

Mr. Cooper said the ruling was a fatal blow to his personal and professional life. The legal bills he incurred have left him bankrupt and out of work.

"I did nothing wrong and tried to point out that the government was intentionally giving set-asides to large companies, and I'm the one who pays for it," Mr. Cooper said. "I wish I'd never done business with the federal government."

7. Richard Pollet, vice president J. Walter Thompson, letter to Joseph Cooper, dated January 16, 2007

Richard Pollet
Executive Vice President
General Counsel

richard.pollet@jwt.com
466 Lexington Avenue, New York, NY 10017
P +1 212 210 6960 F +1 212 210 6852
www.jwt.com

January 16, 2007

Mr. Joseph N. Cooper
501 Blanford Street, #6
Rockville, MD 20850

Dear Mr. Cooper:

Your letter of January 1, 2007 to Bob Jeffrey has been forwarded to me.

In response to your letter, we note that you have had the opportunity to air your complaint within our legal system, first by suing the federal government, and subsequently by suing JWT and other ad agencies. Our judicial system decided against your company in both instances and this properly should be the final word on this matter.

We continue to sharply disagree with any and all assertions by you that JWT has misrepresented itself at any time, or that we have in any way violated the law or the rights of your company. The Court's decision on dismissing your case against JWT and others expressly found that the evidence "negates any claim of fraud against the defendants". Should you persist in claiming that JWT engaged in fraudulent conduct, or take any other action contrary to JWT's rights, we will take all appropriate action. While your letter refers to a proposal of some kind, please be advised that we are not prepared to make or consider any proposal given that the judicial system has spoken on this matter. And I would add that this letter is without waiver of any rights or remedies, all of which are preserved.

We regret that you have experienced financial difficulty and are in poor health, and notwithstanding that we have had our differences from a legal

standpoint, we genuinely wish you a speedy recovery and success in your future business endeavors.

Sincerely,

cc: Bob Jeffrey
        Lewis Trencher

ROGUE AGENCIES:

Through the improper and illegal actions of two federal agencies, the SBA and the INS, JCA, a once-successful small minority company with numerous Fortune 500 clients (such as MCI, Inc.; Blue Cross Blue Shield; E-Systems; and Colgate-Palmolive) that was the recipient of the SBA Minority Service Firm of the Year Award for 1994, has been economically destroyed.

This case is not just about an aggrieved contractor disappointed with a Federal agency's treatment of it or about a contractor's failure to realize its full expectations under a government contract. Rather, this case involves egregious circumstances reflecting the SBA's utter neglect of its statutory duties to an 8(a) contractor and the INS's abuse of contracting authority. The actions of these two agencies are particularly unseemly when viewed in the context of a program designed to assist small, disadvantaged businesses.

The Case discusses the problem of federal government contracts designated for small and women or minority-owned businesses being fraudulently given away to large, multimillion dollar firms. It is based on the author's business, J. Cooper & Associates, a small business that participated in the U.S. Small Business Administration 8(a) program.

JCA acquired an $8-million contract with the former Immigration and Naturalization Service. An INS contracting officer gave the contracts to J. Walter Thompson, Bernard Hodes and CASS Communications, which was neither small nor wholly owned by women or minorities. Cooper took his case to two courts over a 15-year period to fight for justice. His is the first and only case of its type to appear in court regarding fraud in this particular government program.

His blistering exposé will give insight into the significant legal hurdles his business had to clear in order to obtain justice. It shows how government contracting offices and courts ignored long-standing laws and existing regulations. "The Case" is an eye-opening book that will shock small-business owners and educate anyone concerned about government and contracting fraud.

Author:

Cooper has worked inside four United States presidential administrations. During the two Reagan administrations, he was a high-ranking black Republican appointee. He was national director of the Office of Federal Contract Compliance Programs in the Department of Labor. OFCCP rules affected more than 20,000 companies employing over 23 million workers. In January 1987, Cooper resigned his position in protest saying some officials in the Reagan Administration are only paying "lip service" to enforce anti-discrimination laws. During the affirmative action war of 1980s, Cooper played a critical role in keeping OFCCP and affirmative action alive and well.

As an assistant director in the Minority Business Development Agency, U.S. Department of Commerce, Cooper established the first Minority Enterprise Development Week, the largest federally sponsored event on minority enterprise development held yearly. He has traveled extensively throughout Europe, Africa and Asia.

www.ingramcontent.com/pod-product-compliance
Lightning Source LLC
Chambersburg PA
CBHW051325170526
45166CB00002B/683